Cute and Easy
Quilting and Stitching

35 step-by-step projects to decorate the home

CHARLOTTE LIDDLE

CICO BOOKS
LONDON NEW YORK

An imprint of Ryland Peters & Small Ltd

20–21 Jockey's Fields   519 Broadway, 5th Floor
London WC1R 4BW   New York, NY 10012

www.cicobooks.com

10 9 8 7 6 5 4 3 2

Text © Charlotte Liddle 2011
Design and photography © CICO Books 2011

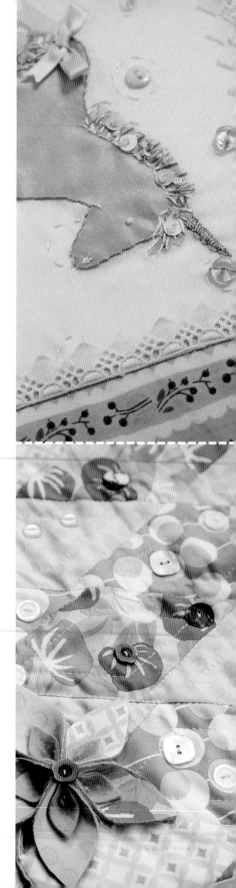

A CIP catalog record for this book is available from the Library of
Congress and the British Library.

ISBN: 978 1 907563 32 4

Printed in China

Editor: Marie Clayton
Designer: Jacqui Caulton
Illustrations: Kate Simunek
Photographer: Penny Wincer
Styling: Alison Davidson

PLEASE READ
Don't mix your measurements. Use
either the imperial or metric, but never
a combination of the two.

Acknowledgments

I would like to thank the team at CICO Books for ensuring
that every element of the book looks great. You have all been
a pleasure to work with.

Contents

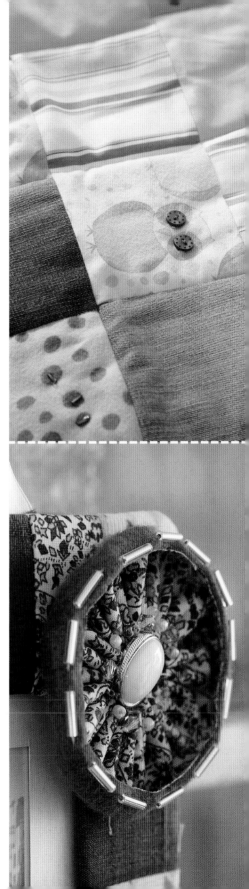

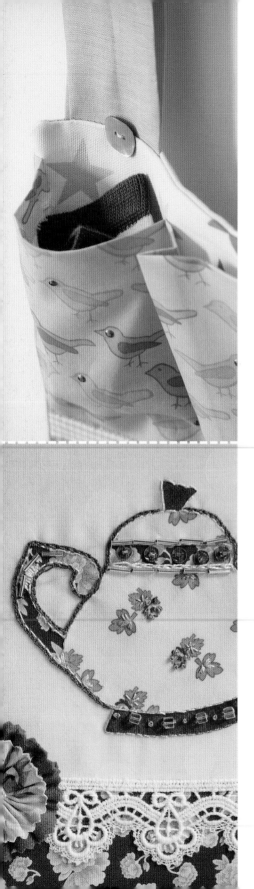

Introduction

The recent hugely successful *Quilts* exhibition at the Victoria and Albert Museum in London helped quilting and patchwork to re-launch its image as a more contemporary form of art. Although the exhibition featured quilts made in the 1700s, it also showed examples of modern textile art by famous artists such as Britain's Tracey Emin. The exhibition was visited by many people, including me, who were inspired to pick up a needle and thread and explore the potential of various quilting techniques. I was particularly excited to develop my patchworking skills and to look for new ways to combine patchwork designs with some of my favorite textile techniques, such as appliqué, embroidery, and embellishment.

With that idea in mind, I approached the publishers with a new book idea that would feature fresh and contemporary projects. *Cute and Easy Quilting and Stitching* was a pleasure to produce. I worked on the 35 projects during the summer months—being inspired by pretty floral fabrics and girly motifs. The book is split into five chapters, starting with *Stitching Know-how*, which explains all the basic stitches. The four projects chapters follow, with each one featuring a collection of designs ranging from simple right through to those that are more intricate.

The *Sweet Dreams* chapter shows you how to make delicate items for your bedroom, such as pajama bags, crib quilts, pillows, and cute dollies. If you love making scrummy items for your kitchen, then chapter 3 *Kitchen Essentials* will be perfect for you; it teaches how to make quirky jam-jar covers, as well as appliquéd egg, tea, and coffee pot cozies.

Many creative people take great pleasure in making beautiful hand-crafted items to give to their friends and family for birthday and Christmas presents. If this sounds like you, then have a look at chapter 4, which is full of *Pretty Gift Ideas*.

The final chapter is entitled *Cute Clothes and Accessories* and is packed with innovative ideas for recycling fabrics and old clothes. Many of the projects utilize small scraps of fabric and suggest ways to incorporate vintage buttons, beads, and sequins into the design.

I had great fun in making this book and thoroughly enjoyed putting into practice some of the new quilting and patchwork techniques that I have learned as a result of visiting the *Quilts* exhibition. I hope you enjoy the book and are inspired to make lots of lovely things, too!

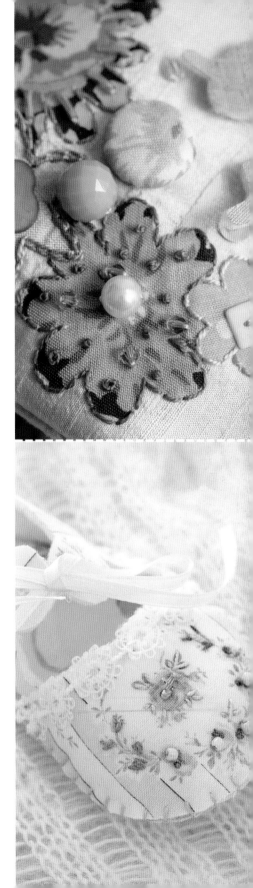

Chapter 1

Stitching Know-how

This section has been put together to explain and demonstrate some of the more general techniques that are used in many of the projects throughout the book. If you have never stitched before, or if you simply need to refresh your memory, then have a good read of the following pages because they will help you to prepare for making textile projects.

Using templates

Many of the projects in this book require some kind of template, whether this is used to make a surface decoration or as a pattern piece.

For projects that need paper templates, simply use tracing paper to copy the template shape from the back of the book. Once copied cut out the template and pin onto fabric.

Depending on how confident you feel, either cut directly around the template shape or draw around it first and then cut it out.

If you are using the templates for an appliqué design, you can draw directly onto the paper side of the Bondaweb instead of using tracing paper.

Appliqué

Appliqué is, without doubt, one of my favorite techniques. It is featured heavily in this book to create some stunning motifs and surface decoration. Bondaweb is a quick and easy way to attach two fabrics together. It helps avoid puckering and fraying edges and keeps your appliqué design flat in preparation for further decorative stitching and embellishment.

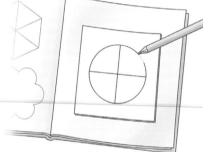

1. Trace the outlines of all the appliqué pieces from the template onto separate areas of the paper backing of a piece of Bondaweb.

2. Cut the Bondaweb tracing into separate pieces.

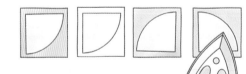

3. Decide on the colour for each part of the design and select the fabrics. Iron each Bondaweb piece onto the back of the corresponding fabric.

4. Cut around the bonded shapes and peel back the paper backing. Build up the appliqué design by placing the pieces Bondaweb side down onto the base fabric. When you are happy with the design, iron all the pieces in place.

Yo-yo

This is another of my favorite techniques. The yo-yo, which is also known as a Suffolk Puff, is a simple gathered circle of fabric that makes a very pretty textured embellishment and can be adapted in many ways for different effects. Traditionally, yo-yos would be made from basic circle shapes, but they can also be cut into with scissors and pinking shears, stuffed, or even made from a heart-shape fabric piece for a more interesting look.

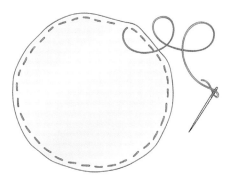

1. Cut out a circle of fabric to approximately twice the finished size that you require. Fold the raw edge under by around ⅛in. (3mm) and work a line of small running stitches around the edge of the circle.

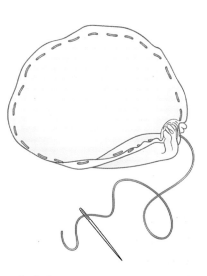

2. Pull on the thread to gather the circle evenly into a puff. Fasten off the thread securely inside the puff to hold the shape in place.

Embroidery

There are so many different hand embroidery stitches it would be impossible to feature them all in this book, so instead I have carefully selected a variety of simple and more decorative stitches that work well on all of the appliqué designs. The great thing about hand embroidery is that you need very little equipment, allowing you to continue working on your project wherever you may be; in the garden, on the train, or even on the beach! Have a go at these stitches and you will be ready to embroider any of the featured projects.

Satin stitch

Work straight stitches very close together, working to the outline of the shape and keeping the edges even. You may prefer to draw the shape onto the fabric first; if so ensure that your stitches are worked to the outside of the line so it does not show on the finished piece.

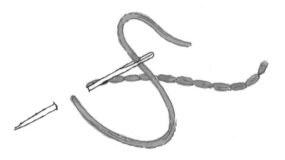

Back stitch

Back stitch is very useful because it gives the effect of a continuous line. Bring the thread up through the fabric then work a stitch backward. Go down through the fabric and underneath, and come up a stitch length in front of the last stitch. Work the next stitch backward to meet the end of the first stitch worked. Repeat to make a continuous line of stitching.

French knots

French knots are created by winding the thread around the needle three times before inserting it back into the fabric right next to where it came out. The French knot sits on the surface of the fabric and should resemble a little bead.

Chain stitch

This is a great stitch for outlining motifs or shapes within an appliqué design. Take a short stitch in the fabric, and make a loop around the tip of the needle with the thread. Take the needle down into the fabric again at the top of the loop to begin the next stitch.

Blanket stitch

Bring the thread out through the fabric at the top of the stitch. Take a vertical stitch through the fabric a short distance away and then loop the thread around the tip of the needle and pull it through. Take the next stitch the same way, making sure the vertical stitches are all the same length and the same distance apart.

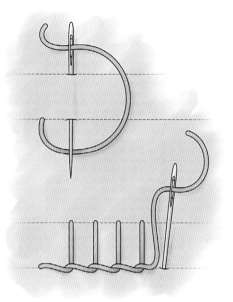

Slip stitch

This is used to stitch two layers of fabric together so that the stitches are almost invisible on the right side. Work a stitch along the fold of the fabric, then a tiny stitch on the other layer making sure it doesn't go through to the front surface.

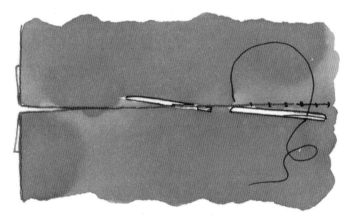

Sewing on beads, sequins, and buttons

To stitch on a sequin with a bead, bring the thread up through the fabric, then thread on the sequin and tiny bead, take the thread over the bead and back down through the hole in the sequin. Single beads are sewn on in the same way, omitting the sequin. To sew on a button, stitch through the holes or through the ring at the back, depending on the button type.

Chapter 2

Sweet Dreams

Crib quilt

Lavender bag

Room tidy with storage pockets

Stuffed dolly

Rosette pillow

Unicorn pillow

Bed runner

Pajama bag

Hanging letters

Crib quilt

I should have called this project "a cheat's guide to patchwork!" If, like me, you are a little impatient, then this is the perfect project for you—it shows you how to use a sewing machine to speed up the patchwork process, but carefully selected fabrics make this look as stunning as traditional hand-crafted quilts.

Materials

8 x 8in. (20 x 20cm) each of four floral design fabrics

8 x 8in. (20 x 20cm) each of two dotted fabrics

8 x 8in. (20 x 20cm) each of two plain fabrics

Heart, butterfly, star, and flower templates on page 118

5 x 6in. (12.5 x 15cm) each of green, blue, silver, and pink silk fabrics

5 x 8in. (12.5 x 20cm) piece of Bondaweb

6 x 20in. (15 x 50cm) each of plain pink and floral fabrics

20 x 24in. (50 x 60cm) piece of striped backing fabric

Embroidery floss (thread)

Sewing machine thread

20 x 24in. (50 x 60cm) piece of batting (wadding)

1. Cut 30 squares each measuring 4 x 4in. (10 x 10cm): 15 squares from floral fabric, eight from the dotted fabric, and seven from the plain fabric. Apply Bondaweb to the back of each of the silk fabrics and use the templates to make four hearts in green silk, four butterflies in blue silk, four stars in silver silk, and three flowers in pink silk.

2. Cut out and apply the motifs onto various plain and dotted fabric squares using the appliqué instructions on page 10. Decorate the motifs with embroidery stitches (see pages 12–13), using the photograph opposite as a guide. Arrange the squares in five rows of six. Using a ¼in. (5mm) seam, stitch the squares together in rows and then stitch the rows together to make the patchwork top.

3. Cut two side borders from plain pink fabric, each 3 x 20in. (7.5 x 50cm), and a top and bottom border from floral fabric each 3 x 20in. (7.5 x 50cm). With right sides facing, pin and stitch the side borders to the patchwork top using a ⅝in. (15mm) seam. Open out and press. Repeat with the top and bottom borders.

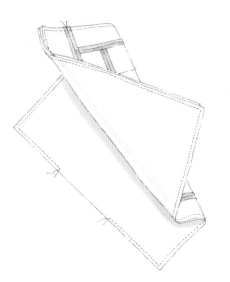

4. Press the seams on the patchwork in alternate directions to minimize bulk. Cut the backing fabric and batting (wadding) to match the finished patchwork top. Place the patchwork top and the backing fabric right sides together and place the batting (wadding) on top. Pin and machine stitch around all edges, leaving a gap for turning.

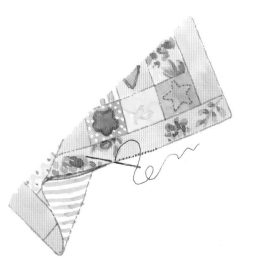

5. Trim the seam and clip corners. Turn the quilt right side out, press and close the gap in the edge seam with slip stitch.

Lavender bag

If you like origami, then you will definitely like this project. The Somerset Star patchwork technique is prefect when making lavender bags because the main part of star is backed with netting to let the scent of the lavender come through—guaranteed to make your linen smell lovely.

Materials

8 x 16in. (20 x 40cm) piece
of floral fabric

6 x 6in (15 x 15cm) piece
of white fine netting

4 x 4in. (10 x 10cm) piece
of green and pink silk

4 x 4in. (10 x 10cm) piece
of Bondaweb

Small pink button

Dried lavender

4in. (10cm) of white
trimming

Small pink ribbon bow

4 heart embellishments

1. Cut eight 4 x 4in. (10 x 10cm) pieces of floral fabric. Fold each of the squares in half wrong sides together with the fold line at the top, and then fold each top corner down to the bottom center to make a triangle. Press in place.

2. Fold the netting in half and press the fold line. Open out and fold in half the other way and then diagonally, pressing each time to create a star of fold lines as a guide for positioning. Arrange a triangle at the center of each side, pointing toward the middle and with the side showing a center join uppermost, and baste (tack) in place.

3. Arrange the remaining four triangles on top and between the first four so their tips align with the sides of the triangles on each side. Baste (tack) in place to make a Somerset Star patchwork.

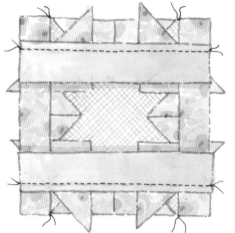

4. Cut four strips of floral fabric each 1¼ x 6in. (3 x 15cm). Pin and sew one strip at the top and one at the bottom first, and then add a strip on either side, using a ¼in. (5mm) seam each time. Press all seams away from the netting and remove the basting (tacking) holding the triangles in place.

5. Cut a 6 x 6in. (15 x 15cm) piece of the floral fabric for the back of the lavender bag. Place front and back together with right sides facing and machine stitch around the edges, using a ¼in. (5mm) seam and leaving a gap in the top for turning. Turn the bag right side out and press.

6. Following the instructions on page 11, make two yo-yos (Suffolk puffs) for decoration, one in pink and one in green silk. Stitch these one on top of the other on the left-hand corner of the lavender bag and top with the pink button.

7. Fill the bag with dried lavender. Insert the ends of a loop of white trimming into the gap, turn the edges under and then hand stitch the gap closed. Stitch a small ribbon bow on top and add heart embellishments to four of the star points.

Room tidy with storage pockets

If you are tired of cleaning up after your children and you need a fun way to organize their toys or stationery, try this great project. Make this lively wall tidy from brightly patterned fabrics, with lots of separate pockets for easy storage of all those odds and ends.

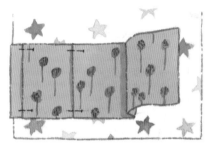

Materials

17 x 7¼in. (42.5 x 18cm) each of three different printed cotton fabrics

14 x 20in. (35 x 50cm) each of star print and polka dot heavy cotton fabric

42in. (105cm) of blue gingham ribbon

5¼ x 20in. (13 x 50cm) piece of plain green fabric

Iron-on rhinestone transfers

2 buttons

1. Turn under the top and bottom edges of one strip of printed cotton by ¼in. (5mm) and stitch in place. Start pinning the strip onto the star print fabric panel so the left-hand side raw edges are aligned and the bottom edge of the strip is approx. 1in. (2.5cm) from the bottom of the panel. Make a ½in. (12mm) vertical tuck in the strip ¾in. (18mm) in from the left-hand edge and pin in place. Make a second ½in. (12mm) vertical tuck 5in. (12.5cm) in from the left-hand edge, and a third 4¾in. (12cm) in from right-hand edge.

2. Repeat step 1 with the other two strips, placing each one with the bottom approx. 1in. (2.5cm) above the top of the one below. Machine stitch vertically ⅛in (3mm) to the left of each tuck across the strips only, and then stitch horizontally across the base of each strip to create individual pockets.

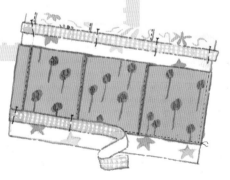

3. Cut the gingham ribbon into three lengths and pin one along the bottom edge of each pocket strip to conceal the bottom seam. Zigzag stitch the ribbon in place.

Tip

The tucks in the strips create extra space in each pocket to store larger items.

4. Fold the length of green fabric in half and stitch along the length. Turn out to make tube, flatten so the seam runs down the center and press. Cut in half to make two tabs. Fold the tabs with the seam on the inside and pin onto the main panel with raw edges aligned and the fold facing downward as shown.

5. Place the polka dot fabric right sides together onto the front of the wall tidy and machine stitch around all edges with a ⅝in. (15mm) seam allowance, leaving a gap in the bottom edge for turning. Turn right side out and press. Turn under the edges of the gap and slip stitch closed. Iron pieces of the rhinestone transfer onto the pockets and stitch buttons onto the tabs.

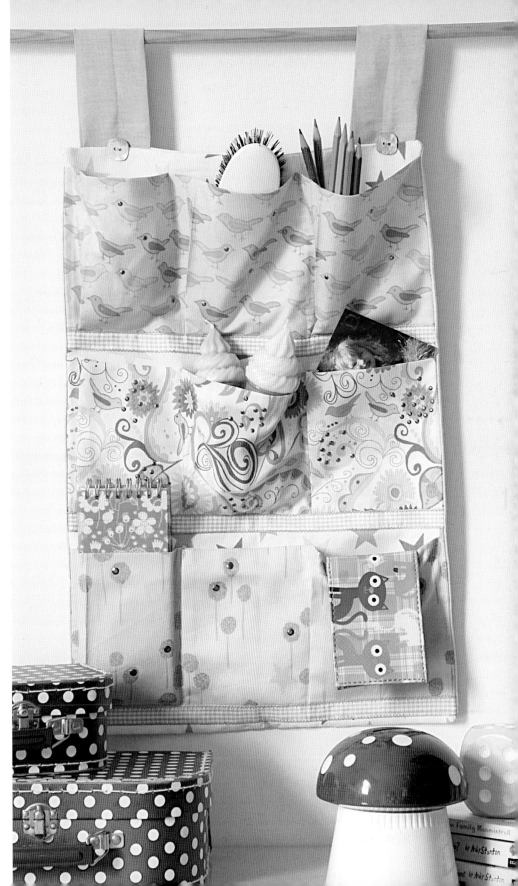

Stuffed dolly

This elegant lady is one of my favorite projects and is definitely not a traditional rag doll—she is far too smart to be made from rags! I had so much fun making the doll, I could have spent hours making different outfits for her. Why not have a go yourself?

1. Copy the doll torso template on page 119 onto the cream linen. Following the appliqué steps as shown on page 10, add the hair in lemon linen and the cheeks in pink silk

2. Cut out around the doll torso. Use the front as a template to cut out a matching piece of white felt for the back of the doll. Embroider the details on the face, adding beading and sequins as described on pages 12–13, and using the photograph opposite as a guide.

3. Using the arm and leg templates, cut four arm shapes and four leg shapes from the cream linen. Place one arm onto another, right sides together, and pin and machine stitch around the shape, using a ¼in. (5mm) seam and leaving the top edge open for turning and stuffing. Turn right side out and press. Repeat for the other arm and the legs. Stuff the arms and legs with fiberfill stuffing.

4. Pin the torso front and back right sides together, inserting the arms at the sides. Blanket stitch around the edge, leaving the bottom of the torso open for stuffing. Stuff the torso, insert the legs in the bottom edge and complete the edge stitching.

Materials

10 x 12in. (25 x 30cm) piece of cream linen fabric

Doll template on pages 118–119

3 x 4in. (7.5 x 10cm) piece of lemon linen fabric

Scrap of pink silk

10 x 12in. (25 x 30cm) piece of Bondaweb

10 x 12in. (25 x 30cm) piece of white felt

Pink and yellow embroidery floss

Beads, sequins, and buttons

Fiberfill stuffing

5 x 16in. (12.5 x 40cm) piece of lilac dotted fabric

3 x 3in. (7.5 x 7.5cm) piece of turquoise silk fabric

Scraps of white and lilac silk fabric

17in. (42.5cm) of wide white trimming

3 x 6in. (7.5 x 15cm) piece of lilac floral fabric

10in. (25cm) of narrow white braid

6in. (15cm) of lemon ribbon

2 x 2in. (5 x 5cm) piece of turquoise spotty fabric

Tiny pink crochet flower

Necklace of tiny beads

6in. (15cm) of narrow pink ribbon

5. Using the skirt template, cut the front and back piece from the lilac dotted fabric. Following the appliqué steps on page 10, create the flower appliqué design. Add embroidery, beading, sequins, and buttons (see pages 12–13), using the photograph (left) as a guide.

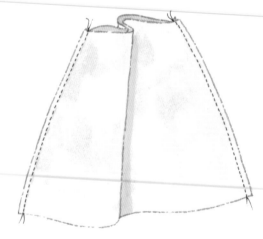

6. With right sides facing, stitch the skirt front to the skirt back at side seams, using a ¼in. (5mm) seam. Turn right side out and press. Machine stitch the wide trimming around the bottom of the skirt.

7. Fold the top edge of the skirt under by ¼in. (5mm), press and machine stitch all around using large stitches. Knot the two threads at one end of the stitching and pull one thread at the other end to gather the skirt to fit the dolly's waist. Hand stitch the skirt onto the torso.

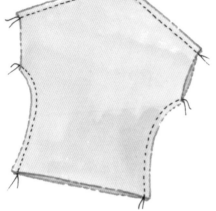

8. Use the blouse template to cut out the front and back pieces. Place the front and back right sides together and machine stitch at the top and side edges, using a ¼in. (5mm) seam.

9. Snip down vertically at the neckline center on one side so the blouse will fit over the head of the dolly. Put the blouse on with the slit at the back and then hand stitch the slit neatly closed.

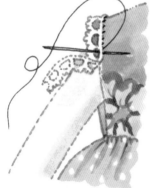

10. Hand stitch a length of the braid around both armholes of the blouse and add a length of yellow ribbon around the dolly's waist.

11. Make a small yo-yo (Suffolk puff) following the instructions on page 11. Add the crochet flower and embellish with buttons. Stitch to the dolly's blouse. Stitch a tiny string of beads around the dolly's neck as a necklace. Tie the pink ribbon into a bow and stitch to the dolly's head.

Rosette pillow

I loved horse riding when I was a little girl, and this pillow takes inspiration from some of my precious rosettes. The subtle blue stripes complement the delicate green spots, creating a color scheme that is understated and fresh.

1. Cut concentric circles from the floral, striped, and dotted fabrics to make up the rosette. Cut a tail from each fabric. Following the appliqué steps as shown on page 10, create the rosette appliqué design on the square of white fabric. Make up a yo-yo (Suffolk puff) in the striped fabric as described on page 11 and add to the center. Add embroidery, beading, and sequins as described on pages 12–13, using the photograph opposite as a guide.

2. Stitch the two coordinating striped fabrics to the top and bottom of the appliqué square using a ¼in. (5mm) seam. Pink the seam allowances and press the seams open. Next cut out a 4 x 18in. (10 x 45cm) piece of floral fabric and stitch this to the right-hand side of the patchwork panel.

3. Cut a 4 x 18in. (10 x 45cm) strip of fine blue stripe fabric and stitch it to the right-hand side of the floral strip. Cut a 14 x 18in. (35 x 45cm) piece of fine blue stripe fabric and stitch this to the left-hand side of the patchwork panel.

4. Follow the instructions to cover the self-cover buttons. Stitch all buttons down one seam of the patchwork panel. For the back cut two 16 x 18in. (40 x 45cm) pieces of fine blue stripe fabric. Make a hem along one short edge of each. Lay these both right side facing on the front panel, overlapping the hemmed edges and aligning raw edges. Stitch all round edges. Turn right side out and insert pillow.

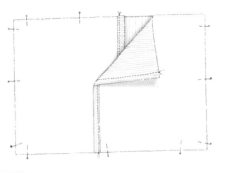

Materials

4 x 18in. (10 x 45cm) piece of floral fabric

4 x 4in. (10 x 10cm) piece of green dotted fabric

7 x 7in. (17.5 x 17.5cm) piece of plain white cotton fabric

4 x 5in. (10 x 12.5cm) piece of Bondaweb

Coordinating pearl embroidery floss

Coordinating beads and sequins

6 x 7in. (15 x 17.5cm) each of two coordinating striped fabrics

18 x 62in. (45 x 135cm) piece of fine blue stripe fabric

Selection of coordinating buttons

2 self-cover buttons

16 x 26in. (40 x 65cm) pillow form

Unicorn pillow

Every little princess should have her very own unicorn pillow! This project combines appliqué and hand embroidery with a simple log cabin patchwork technique to create a pretty pillow. Yo-yos (also known as Suffolk puffs) are used in an innovative way to add the sparkly rosette decoration.

1. Cut four strips each 16 x 3in. (40 x 7.5cm) from the polka dot fabric. Following the appliqué steps as shown on page 10, create the unicorn appliqué design in peach silk on the remaining polka dot fabric. Add embroidery, beading, sequins, and buttons as described on pages 12–13, using the photograph opposite as a guide. Cut the unicorn appliqué piece down to a square 8 x 8in. (20 x 20cm).

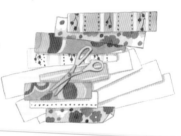

2. Cut one strip 10 x 2in. (25 x 5cm) and another 12 x 3in. (30 x 7.5cm) from each of the four floral fabrics for the log cabin-style patchwork round the appliqué square.

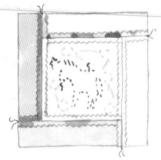

3. Pin the four smaller floral strips around the central unicorn square in a log cabin design as shown left. Machine stitch in place, using a ¼in. (5mm) seam. Repeat with the larger strips of floral fabric, and then with the strips of polka dot fabric. Press all seams flat and neaten the edges with pinking shears.

4. Cut lengths of lemon trimming to fit around the edge of the unicorn square. Pin in place and machine stitch down the middle of the edging. Fold the outer side of the edging in over the stitching and press or hand stitch in place. Cut a circle 5in. (12.5cm) in diameter from the peach silk and make a yo-yo (Suffolk puff) following the instructions on page 11. Cut short lengths of peach ribbon for the tails. Stitch the rosette in place at the corner of the unicorn square.

5. Cut two 19 x 12in. (48 x 30cm) pieces of fabric for the back of the cushion. Follow the instructions on page 28 to construct the envelope back for the cushion and insert the pillow form.

Materials

16 x 22in. (40 x 55cm) piece of lemon polka dot fabric

6 x 12in. (15 x 30cm) piece of peach silk

Unicorn template on page 119

6 x 6in. (15 x 15cm) piece of Bondaweb

Embroidery hoop

Coordinating pearl embroidery floss

Coordinating buttons, beads, and sequins

14 x 6in. (35 x 15cm) each of four floral fabrics

20 x 24in. (50 x 60cm) piece of floral fabric

32in. (80cm) of lemon trimming

Scrap of peach ribbon

18in. (45cm) pillow form

Bed runner

Patchwork is a brilliant way to use up small pieces of fabrics. For this bed runner I cut up a pair of old denim jeans and used them for some of the square patches. When stitched together alongside other blue fabrics, they look very effective.

1. Cut the five different fabrics into 14 squares, each 5 x 5in. (12.5 x 12.5cm). Lay the squares out to form a runner 11 squares long and six squares deep. Using a ¼in. (5mm) seam allowance, stitch the top row of squares together in turn, then the following rows. Press the seams in each row to one side, alternating the direction in each subsequent row to minimize bulk at the seamlines. Stitch the rows together, aligning all seamlines.

2. Following the instructions on page 13, stitch buttons and beads to a number of the patches at random to decorate the bed runner. Use the runner as a template for size and cut a piece of striped fabric for the backing to match and a piece of batting (wadding) very slightly larger.

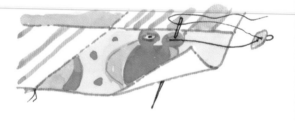

3. Layer the patchwork runner onto the batting (wadding) right side up and machine stitch down each seam to quilt between the pieces.

4. Lay the backing fabric wrong side up and place the patchwork top onto it with the batting (wadding) side downward. Pin and then machine stitch all the way around, using a ¼in. (5mm) seam allowance. Trim the edges to make them equal and straight all around if necessary. Cut the denim fusible binding tape into lengths for each side of the bed runner. Open out the tape and insert the raw edges of the runner, fold back over and iron in place.

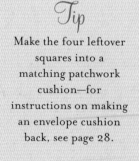

Tip

Make the four leftover squares into a matching patchwork cushion—for instructions on making an envelope cushion back, see page 28.

Pajama bag

Are your favorite pajamas starting to look a little worn out and past their best? If, like me, you can't bear to throw them out, why not cut them up and turn them into a fresh bag for your new pair? This simple drawstring bag is easy to make and will make a great feature for your bed.

1. Cut two 6 x 20in. (15 x 50cm) panels of striped fabric, two 10 x 6in. (25 x 15cm) panels of pink printed fabric, one 20 x 20in. (50 x 50cm) piece of white fabric, and one 10 x 10in. (25 x 25cm) piece of white fabric. Following the appliqué steps as shown on page 10, create the butterfly appliqué design in silk and floral fabric on the smaller square of white fabric. Add embroidery, beading, sequins, and buttons as described on pages 12–13, using the photograph opposite as a guide.

2. Machine stitch the two pink printed pieces onto the top and bottom of the butterfly panel. Press seams open. Add the striped side panels onto each side.

3. Place the front of the bag right sides together to the back and machine stitch around the sides and bottom edge only, leaving a small gap in one side seam 2in. (5cm) from the top edge.

Materials

12 x 20in. (30 x 50cm) piece of striped blue fabric

10 x 12in. (25 x 30cm) piece of pink printed fabric

20 x 30in. (50 x 75cm) piece of plain white fabric

6 x 12in. (15 x 30cm) piece of pink floral fabric

Scraps of blue and pink silk fabric

6 x 10in. (15 x 25cm) piece of Bondaweb

Butterfly templates on page 120

Selection of coordinating pearl embroidery floss

Embroidery hoop

Beads, sequins, and buttons

40in. (100cm) of white ribbon

4. Follow the instructions on page 11 to make a yo-yo (Suffolk puff) in a heart shape . Hand stitch onto the bag and stitch a button into the center.

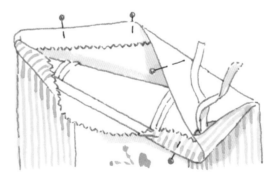

5. Trim the top edge of the bag straight with pinking shears. Fold over the top edge to the inside by 2in. (5cm) and pin the ribbon inside the fold, bringing the ends out to the right side through the gap in the side seam left in step 2. Machine stitch to hold the folded channel in place, taking care not to stitch through the ribbon. Draw up the ribbon and tie the ends into a bow.

Hanging letters

Young children will love these hanging letters. They are simple to make, can be decorated in many ways, and look great hanging from their bedroom door handle. Get the children involved, too, and they can help decorate their very own initial.

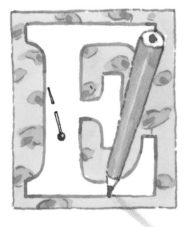

1. Back the floral fabric with the Bondaweb. Place the letter onto the floral side of the fabric, draw around it, and then cut out the letter shape.

Materials

6 x 7in. (15 x 17.5cm) piece of floral fabric

6 x 7in. (15 x 17.5cm) piece of Bondaweb

Letter templates (available from craft stores or print large-scale letters from a computer)

7 x 16in. (17.5 x 40cm) piece of lilac felt

Lilac pearl embroidery floss

Eyelet punch

Approx 30in. (75cm) narrow ribbon

Selection of coordinating buttons

36in. (90cm) wide pink ribbon

Fiberfill stuffing

2. Peel off the Bondaweb backing and place the letter onto a piece of felt. Iron the letter in place and then cut around it leaving an extra ½in. (12mm) border of felt all the way around. Work chain stitch (see page 12) to edge the floral fabric as shown in the photograph opposite.

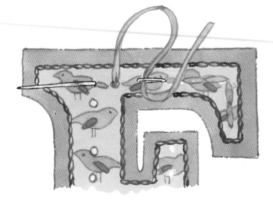

3. Using the eyelet punch, punch holes all the way around the letter spaced around ½in. (12mm) apart. Using back stitch, work ribbon through the holes all around the letter. Stitch on a selection of buttons.

4. Place the letter onto another piece of felt, draw around it and cut out to make an identical letter shape for the back. Place the front piece wrong sides together to the back piece. Fold the wide ribbon in half and insert the ends between the two pieces of felt. Make a few small stitches to hold the ribbon in place on each side.

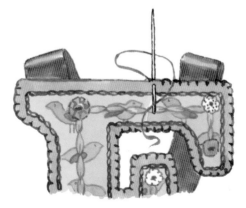

5. Work blanket stitch around the edge, leaving a gap at the top of the letter. Insert the stuffing and then close the gap with blanket stitch.

Chapter 3
Kitchen Essentials

Egg cozy

Jam pot covers

Coffee pot cozy

Doorstop

Teapot picture

Table runner

Apron

Teapot cozy

Egg cozy

This kitsch little egg cozy project is the perfect way to practice your sewing skills. You could make a selection of cozies in different colors—one for each member of the family. You could even embroider initials onto them if you're feeling confident!

Materials

Scraps of different patterned and plain fabrics

10 x 6in. (25 x 15cm) piece of Bondaweb

Octagon template on page 120

4 x 10in. (10 x 25cm) piece of blue cotton fabric

4 x 10in. (10 x 25cm) piece of cotton batting (wadding)

Egg cozy template on page 120

2in. (5cm) of pink ribbon or bias binding

4 x 4in. (10 x 10cm) each of two patterned fabrics

4 x 4in. (10 x 10cm) piece of yellow felt

Small beads

7½in. (19cm) of white trimming

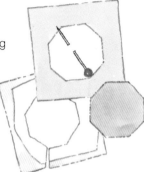

1. Copy the octagon template ten times onto the backing of the Bondaweb. Cut out the Bondaweb octagons and apply to the back of the scraps of patterned fabric, then cut out the shape. Cut a 4 x 5in. (10 x 12.5cm) piece of blue fabric and iron the octagons onto the right side.

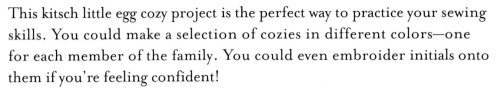

2. Place the octagon appliqué onto the batting (wadding), pin the egg cozy template in place and cut around it through both layers. Repeat with the remaining piece of blue fabric and another layer of batting (wadding).

3. Place the two halves of the cozy right sides together with the batting (wadding) on the outside. Fold the ribbon in half and place it between the layers at top center of the cozy. Machine stitch around the edge, leaving the bottom edge open for turning. Trim seams and turn right side out.

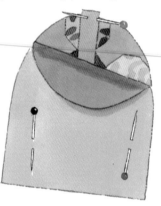

4. Back two different pieces of fabric with yellow felt using Bondaweb. Make two yo-yos (Suffolk puffs) as described on page 11. Cut the back off each to reveal the pleated flower shape inside. Add some beads to the central gathered area of each flower.

5. Stitch the flowers to the top of the egg cozy. Cut a length of white trimming and hand stitch along the bottom of the egg cozy to finish.

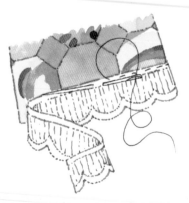

Jam pot covers

These jam jar covers are a great way to use up small pieces of checked or gingham fabrics. Here I have appliquéd strawberry motifs onto the covers, but other fruits such as raspberries and cherries would make great designs.

Materials

6¼ x 12½in. (16 x 32cm) piece of gingham fabric

Strawberry template on page 120

3 x 3in. (7.5 x 7.5cm) each of pink dotted and raspberry silk fabrics

2 x 3in. (5 x 7.5cm) each of green silk and green polka dot fabrics

Coordinating pearl embroidery floss

Coordinating beads and sequins

Embroidery hoop

30in. (75cm) of narrow ribbon

1. Cut the gingham fabric into two squares. Following the appliqué steps as shown on page 10, create the fruit appliqué design in pink and green fabrics in the center of each square.

2. Place each square into an embroidery frame and add embroidery, beading, sequins, and buttons to the appliqué design, as described on pages 12–13. Use the photograph opposite as a guide.

3. Use a pair of pinking shears to cut a circle at least 6¼in. (16cm) in diameter around each appliqué design—the zigzag edge will stop the fabric from fraying. Tie each cover over a jam pot using a length of narrow ribbon.

Coffee pot cozy

This girly coffee pot cozy is the ultimate accessory for those frothy coffee and cupcake mornings! The combination of sweet floral fabrics, white cotton trimming, frills, and flounces takes its inspiration from nostalgic country cafés. The cupcake appliqué defines the word cute—it's yummy and mouthwateringly scrummy.

1. Following the appliqué steps shown on page 10, create the cupcake appliqué design in pink and green on the white cotton fabric. Add embroidery, beading, and sequins as described on pages 12–13, using the photograph opposite as a guide. Cut the cupcake appliqué piece down to 4¾ x 5¼in. (12 x 13cm).

2. Use the triangle template to cut out two triangle patches from each of the four different floral fabrics. Using ¼in. (5mm) seam allowances, stitch one set of triangles together to form a patchwork square as shown, made up of four different triangular fabrics. Repeat to make another square.

3. With raw edges aligned, baste (tack) a length of white broderie anglaise trimming on each side of the cupcake piece so it will be stitched into the seam. Pin one patchwork square to either side of the cupcake appliqué piece, right sides together. Machine stitch all of the pieces together. Remove basting (tacking).

Materials

6 x 6in. (15 x 15cm) piece of white cotton fabric

Scraps of patterned fabric in pink

3 x 3in. (7.5 x 7.5cm) piece of green fabric

Cupcake template on page 121

6 x 6in. (15 x 15cm) piece of Bondaweb

Coordinating pearl embroidery floss

Coordinating beads and sequins

Embroidery hoop

5 x 7in. (12.5 x 17.5cm) each of four floral fabrics

Triangle template on page 121

10in. (25cm) of white broderie anglaise trimming

15 x 6in. (37.5 x 15cm) piece of patterned cotton

14 x 5in. (35 x 12.5cm) piece of cotton batting (wadding)

6½ x 9½in. (16.5 x 24cm) piece of pink dotted fabric

14in. (35cm) of white braid trimming

Eyelet punch

66in. (165cm) of narrow ribbon

4. Cut a 14 x 6in. (35 x 15cm) piece of patterned fabric for the back of the cozy and a 12½ x 4¾in. (32 x 12cm) piece of batting (wadding). Layer the batting (wadding) between the patchwork front and the back, with right sides outermost, and pin in place. Stitch along all the seam lines of the patchwork to quilt the coffee pot cozy.

5. To make the flounce (frill), cut a spiral length of fabric ½in. (12mm) wide and approx. 28in. (70cm) long from the pink spotted fabric as shown. Cut the length of spiral strip in half to make two lengths of flounce (frill). From the same pink spotted fabric, mark and cut two binding strips measuring 14 x 1½in. (35 x 4cm) and two measuring 6½ x 1½in. (16.5 x 4cm). Turn under ¼in. (5mm) along both long edges of all four binding strips.

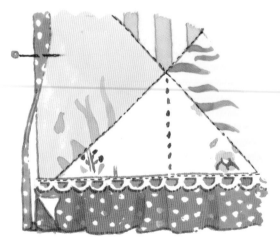

6. Use the two longer binding strips to bind the top and bottom edges of the cozy, as described on page 33. Machine stitch the two lengths of flounce (frill) along the bottom of the front of the cozy. Pin and then machine stitch a length of white braid trimming to conceal the stitching and the top edges of the flounce. Use the shorter binding strips to bind the side edges, catching the ends of the flounce in the binding at each side.

7. Use an eyelet punch to make circular holes at the top and bottom of each side of the cozy just inside the binding. Cut the ribbon into four equal pieces and thread a length through each hole, knotting in place to secure. Wrap the cozy around the coffee pot and tie the ribbons to hold the cozy in place.

Doorstop

The traditional cathedral window technique is currently one of my favorites—this doorstop project is a simple way for you to practice making cathedral window patches before you move on to larger and more complicated designs. I simply love the effect of such a traditional technique worked with modern and vibrant patterned fabrics.

1. Follow the instructions on page 78 to make the cathedral window panel, using two 6 x 6in. (15 x 15cm) squares of blue linen and seven 1½ x 1½in. (4 x 4cm) squares of patterned fabrics. Add a button to the center of each cathedral window.

2. Cut two pieces of red floral fabric 2 x 4in. (5 x 10cm) for each side of the cathedral window panel, a piece 3¼ x 9in. (8 x 22.5cm) for the top and one 5 x 9in. (12.5 x 22.5cm) for the bottom. With right sides facing, and using a ¼in. (5mm) seam, stitch the side pieces to the cathedral window panel. Press seams toward the patchwork.

3. With right sides facing, stitch on the top and bottom pieces in the same way. Open out, press the seams as before and trim any excess. Use the patchwork front as a template to cut a piece for the back of the bag from the red floral fabric.

Materials

12 x 6in. (30 x 15cm) piece of blue linen fabric

1½ x 1½in. (4 x 4cm) each of seven coordinating patterned fabrics

2 buttons

9 x 22in. (22.5 x 55cm) piece of red floral fabric

20in. (50cm) ribbon

4. With right sides facing pin and stitch the front to the back, using a ⅝in. (15mm) seam and leaving the top edge open. Trim the corners, turn the bag right side out, and press. Turn the top edge to the inside twice by approx. ¼in. (5mm) each time and machine stitch to hold in place.

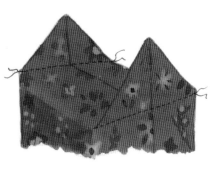

5. To make the gusset, flatten the bag across the corners so the seamline is positioned in the center of the resulting triangle. Measure in 2½in. (6.5cm) from each corner along the seam and stitch across the corner at this point to make a triangular flap. Fold the triangular flaps out to make a flat base. Fill the bag with rice or dried pulses. Gather the top together and tie closed with a ribbon bow.

Teapot picture

Celebrate your love for tea by making this appliquéd and embroidered teapot picture. Hang it alongside your pots and pans or give it as a gift to a fellow tea lover!

1. Following the appliqué steps shown on page 10, create the teapot appliqué design in scraps of floral printed and pink floral fabric on the cream polka dot fabric. Add embroidery, beading, and sequins as described on pages 12–13, using the photograph opposite as a guide.

2. Cut a piece of pink floral fabric 12 x 4in. (30 x 10cm). Pin onto the bottom of the teapot appliqué panel with right sides facing and machine stitch in place. Open out and press seams open. Machine stitch a length of white decorative trimming on top of the pink floral panel.

3. Following the instructions on page 11 make two yo-yos (Suffolk puffs), one from felt and one from the pink floral fabric. Cut the back off each yo-yo using pinking shears to reveal the pleated inside.

4. Place the small flower onto the larger flower, hand stitch the two together and stitch a button in the center. Hand stitch the flower to the appliqué picture.

Materials

4 x 4in. (10 x 10cm) piece of floral printed fabric

12 x 12in. (30 x 30cm) piece of pink floral fabric

10 x 10in. (25 x 25cm) piece of Bondaweb

Teapot template on page 121

12 x 12in. (30 x 30cm) cream polka dot fabric

Coordinating pearl embroidery floss

Embroidery hoop

Selection of beads and sequins

12in. (30cm) of lace trimming

5 x 5in. (12.5 x 12.5cm) of pink felt

2 small buttons

8 x 8in. (20 x 20cm) canvas picture frame

Staple gun

12in. (30cm) of pink ribbon or bias binding

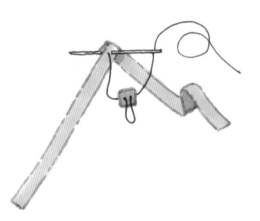

5. Stretch the appliqué picture around the canvas frame and use a staple gun to secure the fabric on the back. Attach ribbon for hanging to the back of the canvas using the staple gun. Strengthen the top of the hanging ribbon by stitching on a button.

Table runner

For me, there has always been something very comforting about lavender, so I designed this table runner with a quaint cottage kitchen in mind. The subtle embroidery and delicate colors would sit perfectly alongside a pot of soothing tea and a plate of homemade cookies.

Materials

22 x 21in. (55 x 52cm) piece of lilac dotted fabric

16 x 21in. (40 x 52cm) piece of lilac floral fabric

5 x 5in. (12.5 x 12.5cm) piece of green silk fabric

2 x 5in. (5 x 12.5cm) piece of lilac silk fabric

6 x 6in. (15 x 15cm) piece of Bondaweb

9 x 21in. (22 x 52cm) piece of plain lilac linen fabric

Beads and sequins

Lilac embroidery floss

Embroidery hoop

27in. (68cm) of lilac ribbon

4 large mother-of-pearl buttons

14 x 60in. (35 x 152cm) piece of backing fabric

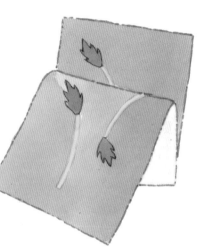

1. Following the appliqué steps shown on page 10, create a lavender flower appliqué design on the piece of plain lilac linen using the photographs opposite as a guide. Add embroidery, beads, and sequins as described on pages 12–13, and work machine zigzag down the stems.

2. Cut two pieces from the lilac dotted fabric each 7 x 21in. (17.5 x 52cm). With right sides facing and using ¼in. (5mm) seams, machine stitch a piece of lilac dotted fabric to either end of the linen appliqué to create the long central panel. Open out and press seams flat.

3. Cut the floral fabric into four strips each 4 x 21in. (10 x 52cm). Cut two strips from the lilac dotted fabric the same size. With right sides facing and using ¼in. (5mm) seams, machine stitch a strip of lilac floral to either end of each lilac dotted strip. Press seams flat. Stitch the dotted/floral strips to either side of the central panel, matching seams. Press seams flat.

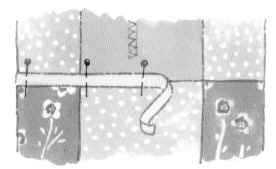

4. Cut the length of ribbon in half and pin the lengths across the runner to cover the seams between the center section and the two end sections. Stitch in place using an open zigzag stitch.

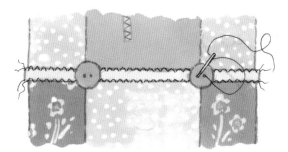

5. Stitch a mother-of-pearl button onto the ribbon at each corner of the different sections of the appliqué panel.

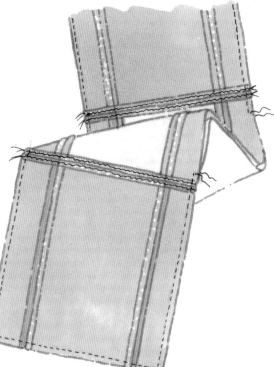

6. Place the backing fabric onto the runner with right sides facing. Machine stitch around all edges using a ¼in. (5mm) seam, and leaving a gap in one side for turning through.

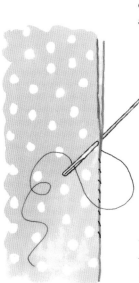

7. Turn the runner right side out and press. Turn the edges of the opening inside and slip stitch the gap closed.

Apron

With beautiful stripes and fresh sunny colors featuring a delicious cherry-topped ice cream, this apron project is definitely fun, frivolous, and guaranteed to make you smile! This project gives you the opportunity to mix patterns in a crazy patchwork style.

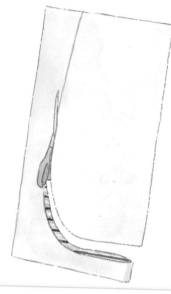

1. To make the basic apron, cut two pieces of striped fabric 18 x 18in. (45 x 45cm). Fold one piece in half and cut the raw edges into a gentle curve outward to create the apron shape, and round off the bottom corner. Use this piece as a template to cut the second piece the same. For the waistband tie cut a length of pink linen fabric 60in x 4¾in. (152 x 12cm). Fold it in half and stitch across each short end and then along the long side toward the center, leaving a 16in. (40cm) gap (or to fit the width of the top of the apron) in the seam in the center of the long side. Turn the waistband tie right side out and press.

2. Following the appliqué steps as shown on page 10, create the ice-cream cone appliqué design in the scraps of pink and yellow on part of the white cotton fabric. Add beading, sequins, and embroidery as described on pages 12–13, using the photograph opposite as a guide. Cut the ice-cream cone appliqué piece down to 3¼ x 5¼in. (8 x 13cm).

Materials

20 x 40in. (50 x 100cm) piece of striped fabric

60in x 4¾in. (150 x 12cm) piece of pink linen

10 x 16in. (25 x 40cm) piece of white cotton

Scraps of pink and yellow linen and silk

Ice cream template on page 122

10 x 16in. (25 x 40cm) piece of Bondaweb

Beads and sequins

Embroidery floss

Embroidery hoop

Pieces of floral and plain fabric

Metallic thread

Buttons and bow

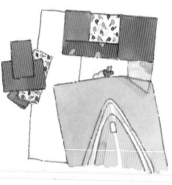

3. Cut a piece of white cotton 8 x 9½in. (20 x 24cm) as a base for the crazy patchwork pocket. Apply Bondaweb to the back of the ice cream appliqué piece and to a selection of random scraps of linen and silk to fit around the appliqué and make up the pocket. Peel off the paper backing and iron the patches onto the white cotton base in turn, using parchment or an ironing cloth to protect the silk pieces.

4. Set the sewing machine to a close zigzag stitch and then stitch around the edges of each piece using metallic pink thread. Add buttons and a bow to decorate, using the photograph opposite as a guide.

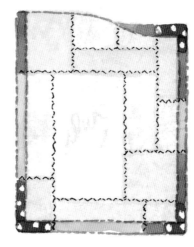

5. Fold the sides and bottom edges under, press and then baste (tack) in place. Fold the top edge of the pocket under, press, and zigzag stitch in place. Pin the pocket onto the apron and zigzag stitch along the sides and bottom edge.

6. Place the front and back apron pieces together with right sides facing and machine stitch around the edges, leaving the top edge open for turning. Turn the apron right side out and press.

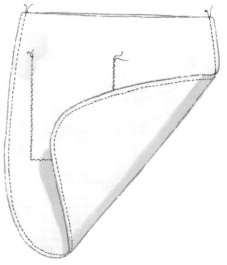

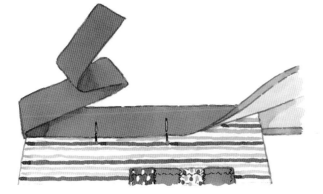

7. Place the top edge of the apron into the gap left in the center bottom seam of the waistband tie. Fold the edges of the gap under neatly on both sides, press and pin in place. Edge stitch along the base of the waistband tie to attach it to the apron.

Teapot cozy

This pretty tea cozy features traditional square patchwork and gorgeously quirky appliqué and embroidery. The tea cup motif is a real focal point and brings the differently colored patches together. And let's not forget the pom pom—how sweet is that?!

1. Cut five 4 x 4in. (10 x 10cm) squares from the green polka dot, pink cotton, floral, and gingham fabrics. Machine stitch the squares together in rows, using a ¼in. (5mm) seam. Stitch the rows together to make a piece of patchwork fabric five squares wide by four squares high.

2. Cut the batting (wadding) in half and lay both pieces on top of the wrong side of the remaining gingham fabric. Add the patchwork fabric on top, right side upward. Pin the teapot cozy template onto all the layers and cut out the teapot cozy shape.

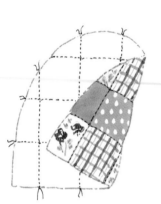

3. Pin the patchwork piece to one piece of the cotton batting (wadding), and machine stitch along the seams of the squares to give a subtle padded effect.

4. Following the appliqué steps shown on page 10, create the teacup appliqué design in floral and pink fabric on the piece of white cotton. Add embroidery, beading, sequins, and buttons as described on pages 12–13, using the photograph opposite as a guide.

Teapot cozy template on page 121

Teacup template on page 121

Materials

- 16 x 20in. (40 x 50cm) piece of green polka dot fabric
- 16 x 24in. (40 x 60cm) each of light pink cotton and floral fabrics
- 16 x 32in. (40 x 80cm) piece of gingham fabric
- 14 x 24in. (35 x 60cm) piece of cotton batting (wadding)
- Teapot cozy template on page 121
- 4 x 5in. (10 x 12.5cm) white cotton fabric
- 4 x 10in. (10 x 25cm) of Bondaweb
- Teacup template on page 121
- Coordinating pearl embroidery floss
- Coordinating beads and sequins
- Embroidery hoop
- 18in. (45cm) thin white braid
- 27in. (68cm) wide trimming
- Two 2 x 2in. (5 x 5cm) pieces of firm cardstock (cardboard)
- Small ball of yellow wool

5. Iron Bondaweb to the back of the teacup appliqué piece and apply it to the center of the patchwork piece. Machine stitch thin white braid around the edge of the appliqué piece to finish off and hide any raw edges.

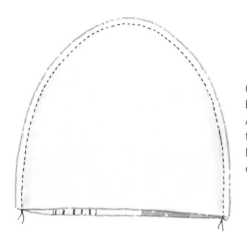

6. With right sides together place the gingham back piece on top of the patchwork front piece. Add the final layer of cotton batting (wadding) on top of the gingham fabric and pin in place. Machine stitch around the edge leaving the bottom edge open for turning.

7. Turn the cozy right side out and press. Machine stitch a length of wide trimming around the bottom edge of the teapot cozy to hide the raw edges.

8. Cut the pieces of cardstock (cardboard) into two circles and cut a smaller circle from the center of each. Place them together and wind the yellow wool around and through the central hole until it is full. Slide a sharp pair of scissors between the layers of cardstock (cardboard) and cut through the yarn all around the edge. Ease the cardstock circles apart and tie a length of yarn firmly around the center to hold all the yarn lengths together. Slide the cardstock (cardboard) away and fluff up the pompom. Trim any odd long ends so it is even. Stitch onto the center top of the teapot cozy.

Chapter 4

Pretty Gift Ideas

Plush Russian doll

Pincushion

Bunting

Embroidered picture

Embroidered brooch

Book cover

Picture frame

Shoe bag

Coin purse

Plush Russian doll

This is one of my favorite projects; like many people, I love the charm of Russian dolls. This appliqué picture is simple to make (making it a good way to practice the appliqué technique) and would make a great present for friends young or old!

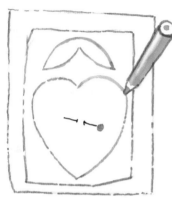

1. Trace the outlines of all the Russian doll piece templates onto separate areas of the piece of Bondaweb. Make a duplicate copy of the hair and the heart onto a separate piece of bondaweb. Cut the Bondaweb tracing of the doll into its individual pieces. Fold the piece of pale lilac felt in half and cut it into two pieces.

2. Select the pieces of fabric for the individual parts of the Russian doll. Iron the corresponding Bondaweb piece onto the back of each piece. Cut around each shape and peel off the paper backing. Repeat this for all the segments.

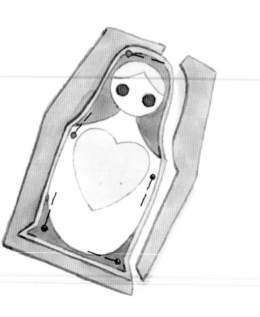

3. Build up the appliqué doll by placing all the individual segments onto one side of one piece of the pale lilac felt, Bondaweb side down. When you are happy with the design iron all the pieces in place. Cut around the doll shape leaving approx ¼in. (5mm) extra fabric all around the edge for the seam allowance. Use the cut-out shape to cut a second piece of felt for the doll back.

Materials

Doll template on page 122

10 x 10in. (25 x 25cm) piece of Bondaweb

10 x 6in. (25 x 15cm) piece of pale lilac felt

7 x 5in. (17.5 x 12.5cm) piece of dark lilac linen

4 x 5in. (10 x 12.5cm) piece of pale lemon plain linen

5 x 6in. (12.5 x 15cm) piece of white silk fabric

3 x 3in. (7.5 x 7.5cm) piece of cream cotton fabric

Scrap of pink silk fabric

5 x 5in. (7.5 x 7.5cm) piece of lilac floral fabric

Pearl embroidery floss

Beads and sequins

Short length of pink ribbon

6in. (15cm) of lilac ribbon

Fiberfill stuffing

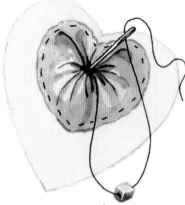

4. Create a heart shape yo-yo (Suffolk puff) using the lilac floral fabric and following the instructions on page 11. Stitch this into the center of the yellow linen heart shape on the doll. Add embroidery to decorate the Russian doll appliqué following the instructions on pages 12–13 and using the photograph opposite as a guide.

5. Use the template as a guide for stitching the facial features. Add beads and sequins to the outer areas of the doll, following the instructions on page 13 and using the photograph as a guide. Make a small bow in the pink ribbon and attach to the doll's head as a hair decoration.

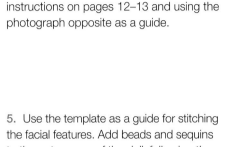

6. Place the appliquéd front doll piece on top of the plain backing felt piece and pin in place. Insert a loop of gingham ribbon into the top of the doll between the layers and pin. Work a short line of running stitch to hold the loop in place.

7. Work blanket stitch all around the edge of the doll, leaving the bottom edge open for stuffing. Insert fiberfill stuffing into the doll at the base to firm out the shape and then close the gap using blanket stitch.

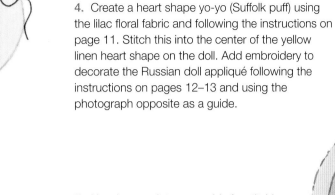

Pincushion

I had cupcakes in mind when I was designing this pincushion. Yo-yos (Suffolk puffs) are used to make the main part of the cushion, with simple fabric rose embellishments as decoration. If you are always losing your pincushion while you work, why not attach a wrist strap and make it wearable?!

Materials

5 x 10in. (12.5 x 25cm) each of eight coordinating fabrics

Fiberfill stuffing

12in. (30cm) piece of white lace

16in. (40cm) piece of white trimming

5 x 10in. (12.5 x 25cm) piece of lilac felt

5 x 5in. (12.5 x 12.5cm) piece of pink felt

5 x 15in. (12.5 x 37.5cm) piece of pink silk

5 x 15in. (12.5 x 37.5cm) piece of Bondaweb

3 pearls

Beads and sequins

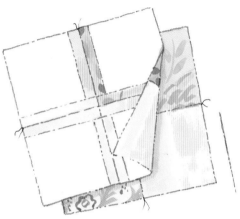

1. Cut two 5 x 5in. (12.5 x 12.5cm) squares from each of the eight coordinating fabrics. Stitch four squares together, using a ¼in. (5mm) seam, to create a large patchwork square. Repeat with the remaining four squares.

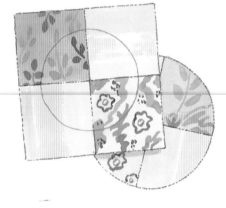

2. Mark a circle 8in. (20cm) in diameter onto one of the patchwork squares, draw around it and cut out. Repeat on the other patchwork square, but marking a circle 6in. (15cm) in diameter.

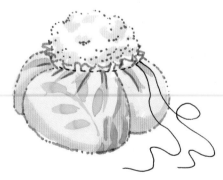

3. Follow the instructions on page 11 to make each circle into a yo-yo (Suffolk puff). Before fully tightening the gathering to close up the center hole, stuff each firmly with fiberfill. Tighten the gathering and secure.

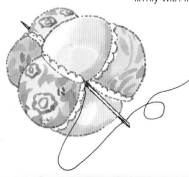

4. Cut and stitch two lengths of white lace around the smaller yo-yo (Suffolk puff) and white trimming around the larger one, positioned as if wrapping a gift. Stitch the small yo-yo (Suffolk puff) on top of the larger one.

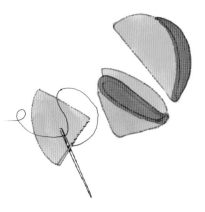

5. Use the Bondaweb to bond pink silk to one side of the lilac felt and one side of the pink felt. Cut one circle for each flower from the lilac felt/silk. Fold each circle in half with the silk on the outside, and then fold in half again. Stitch the folded edges together. Open out the center to form a cone-shape flower and stitch pearl beads into the cone. Repeat to make the other flowers.

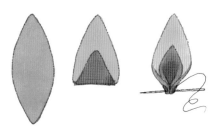

6. Cut out a leaf shape from the pink felt/silk and fold the end over crossways. Fold in half along the length, and then stitch the short folded edges together to hold in place. Stitch the flowers and leaves to the top of the pincushion using the photograph opposite as a guide. For extra sparkle sew on beads and sequins randomly.

Bunting

Bunting is always popular—it's a great way to add an injection of color and pattern to bedroom and is a fabulous and fun gift you can bring to help decorate a party. This row of sweet bunting is strung onto white cotton decorative trimming.

Materials

8 x 20in. (20 x 50cm) each of eight coordinating fabrics

Bunting template on page 122

100in. (250cm) of wide cotton trimming

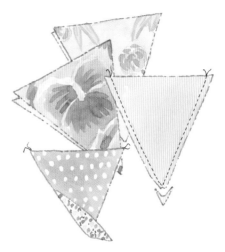

1. Using the bunting template, cut three triangles from each of the eight fabrics. These 24 triangles will create approx. 100in. (250cm) of bunting. Place two triangles together with right sides facing, mixing fabrics and designs. Machine stitch along the sides using a ¼in. (5mm) seam allowance, leaving the top edge open. Trim off the point of the triangle, being careful not to cut through the stitching. Turn right side out and press. Repeat for all the triangles.

2. Fold the length of cotton trimming in half along the length and press. Insert the top edge of each triangle into the folded trimming, leaving a gap of around 4in. (10cm) between each triangle. Pin the triangles in place.

Tip

If you want to tie up the bunting at each end, start with a 36in. (90cm) longer length of trimming and space the end flags at least 18in. (45cm) in from the end on each side. Position the other flags equally between the two end ones.

3. Turn the ends of the cotton trimming in to neaten them, aligning with the side of the final triangle at each end. Machine stitch all along the trimming, making sure you catch the tops of the triangles in the seam to attach them.

Embroidered picture

This is another project featuring the ever-popular Russian dolls! Make as many dolls as you need to fill the width of your picture, or make several in different sizes.

1. Following the appliqué steps shown on page 10, create the Russian doll appliqué design in the scraps of fabric on the blue linen. Add embroidery, beading, sequins, and buttons as described on pages 12–13, using the photograph opposite as a guide.

2. Stretch the appliquéd fabric around the canvas picture frame and fix it in place using the staple gun.

3. Run a length of floral trimming along the bottom of the canvas and use the staple gun to attach it at the back on each side.

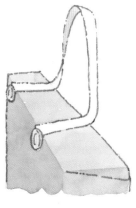

4. Use the glue gun to attach the ends of the ribbon to the top of the canvas, coming slightly over onto the front as shown in the photograph opposite. Use the hot glue gun to attach the two large buttons onto the front to hide the ends of the ribbon.

Materials

Selection of blue, red, and pink plain and patterned fabrics

10 x 10in. (25 x 25cm) piece of Bondaweb

12 x 12in. (30 x 30cm) blue linen fabric

Russian doll templates on page 123

Beads, sequins, bows, and buttons

Coordinating embroidery floss

Embroidery hoop

8 x 8in. (20 x 20cm) canvas picture frame

Staple gun

12in. (30cm) of floral trimming

15in. (37.5cm) of ribbon

2 large pink buttons

Hot glue gun

Embroidered brooch

Birds are very much in fashion—you will see them as motifs on wallpapers and fabrics, as hanging decorations, and even as brooches. This stuffed appliqué bird brooch could easily be turned into an individual hanging decoration, or if you make several, you could to hang from a mobile.

1. Copy the bird template and follow the appliqué steps shown on page 10, to create the bird appliqué design in scraps of silk on half the light pink felt.

2. Decorate the bird by adding embroidery, beading, and sequins as described on pages 12–13, using the photographs opposite as a guide. Cut out the bird shape, leaving a little extra all around for a seam.

3. Draw and cut out an identical bird shape for the back of the brooch from the remaining pink felt. Place the two pieces wrong sides together and work blanket stitch all around the edge of the brooch, leaving a small gap to stuff. Insert the stuffing and carry on working in blanket stitch to close the gap.

4. Make three small loops from blue ribbon for tail feathers and stitch a button to secure in place. Stitch the brooch pin to the back of the bird.

Book cover

If you have books with uninspiring covers, or special notebooks or diaries that could do with a makeover, this project will be perfect for you. It is a slight development from the doorstop project on page 48, as it features four cathedral window patches instead of two, but the end result is certainly worth the work.

on page 48

Materials

12 x 12in. (30 x 30cm) piece of red linen fabric

5 x 6½in. (12.5 x 16.5cm) each of two floral and two dotted fabrics

5 red buttons

6 x 12in. (15 x 30cm) piece of dotted fabric

14 x 12in. (35 x 30cm) piece of floral fabric

1 large sparkly button

Short length of narrow ribbon

1. Cut four squares of red linen fabric each measuring 6 x 6in. (15 x 15cm). Cut 12 small squares from the four patterned fabrics, each measuring 1½ x 1½in. (4 x 4cm). Take one of the red linen squares and fold each of the corners into the center point and press. Fold each corner into the center point again; press and pin in place. Work a couple of stitches into the center to hold the points in place. Repeat for each of the four squares.

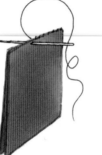

2. Slip stitch the four folded squares together into one big square working from the reverse side.

3. Place a small square of patterned fabric diagonally over each seam and pin in place. Place the remaining eight patterned squares diagonally over the edges of the panel, two on each side.

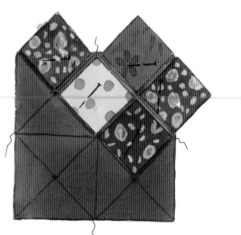

4. Turn back the folded edges of the red linen over the raw edges of the patterned squares to create a curved frame and stitch in place. Repeat with all the squares. Trim off any points of patterned fabric that extend past the edges of the main patchwork piece.

5. Stitch a button into the center of each of the cathedral windows.

6. Cut a piece of floral fabric 7 x 10in. (17.5 x 25cm) for the back and two pieces 6½ x 3in. (16.5 x 7.5cm) for the top and bottom border of the cathedral window panel. Cut a piece of dotted fabric 2 x 10in. (5 x 25cm) for the spine, and one 3 x 10in. (7.5 x 25cm) for the front inner panel. With right sides facing pin the top and bottom pieces to the cathedral window panel and machine stitch in place. Open out and press the seam.

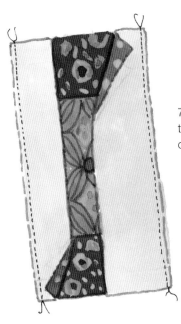

7. With right sides together pin and stitch the spine piece and the right inner piece onto the front cathedral window panel.

8. With right sides together pin and sew the back piece to the front piece. Press seams and trim raw edges with pinking shears. Press all edges under by ½in. (12mm) all around or to fit the book.

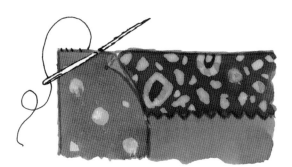

9. Place the book into the cover and fold the excess fabric on either side over to make a flap. Slip stitch at top and bottom to hold the flap in place.

10. Stitch the large sparkly button onto the front of the book. Create a ribbon loop to fit over the button and stitch onto the inside flap at the back of the book.

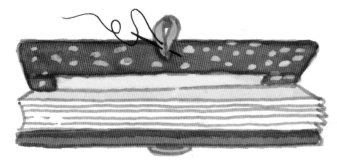

Picture frame

I am very nostalgic and always love looking through old black-and-white family photos. They are so very charming and I believe that they deserve to be framed in something a little bit special. Choose scraps of your favorite fabrics (or even use vintage fabrics) to make a gorgeous vintage-style frame for your own precious photograph.

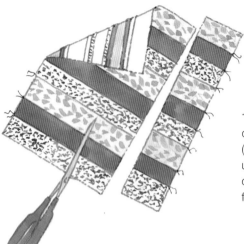

1. Cut two strips of fabric from each of the different patterns, all around 1½ x 10in. (4 x 25cm). Pin and stitch these strips together using a ¼in. (5mm) seam to make a striped piece of fabric. Cut the piece of striped patchwork into four lengths.

Materials

3¼ x 10in. (8 x 25cm) each of floral, printed baby cord, and raspberry silk fabrics

7¼ x 8¾in. (18 x 22cm) piece of cardstock (cardboard)

Hot glue gun

Masking tape

10in. (25cm) of cream ribbon

7¼ x 8¾in. (18 x 22cm) piece of thick cardstock (cardboard)

6 x 6in. (15 x 15cm) piece of floral fabric

6 x 6in. (15 x 15cm) piece of Bondaweb

6 x 6in. (15 x 15cm) piece of pink felt

Beads, sequins, and vintage button

2. Make a base frame in cardstock (cardboard) measuring 7¼ x 8¾in. (18 x 22cm) with a 1½in. (4cm) wide border.

3. Cut two of the strips of patchwork fabric down to 8⅜in. (21cm) in length. Cut the ends of all four strips across diagonally as shown.

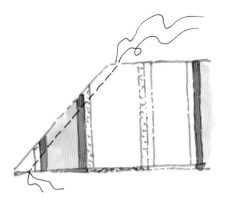

4. With right sides facing, pin each of the pieces together. Machine stitch in place but do not back stitch at the start and end of any of the seams. Trim and press the seams open.

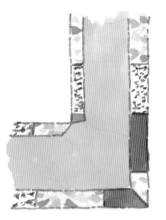

5. Place the fabric over the cardstock (cardboard) frame, undoing a few stitches at the end of each seam as necessary so the fabric fits the frame neatly. Use either a hot glue gun or masking tape to secure the fabric around the frame.

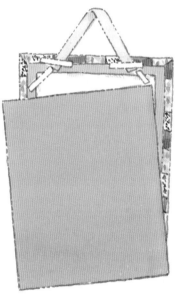

6. Place the picture behind the frame, securing in place with masking tape. Tape the length of ribbon for hanging in place. Use the hot glue gun to attach the piece of thick cardstock (cardboard) on the back of the frame.

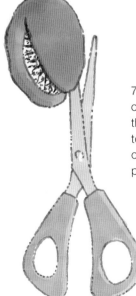

7. Iron the Bondaweb onto the back of the square of floral fabric. Remove the paper backing and iron the felt on top. Follow the instructions on page 11 to make a yo-yo (Suffolk puff) with the felt on the outside. Cut out the back of the yo-yo to reveal the pleated inside.

8. Apply beads, sequins, and a vintage button to the yo-yo (Suffolk puff) to embellish the flower. Use the hot glue gun to attach it onto the frame.

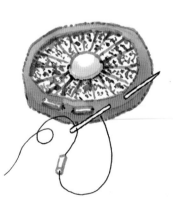

Shoe bag

I know so many girls who, like me, love to collect shoes. So if you are a shoe addict, then you must make yourself this bag and use it to carry around your party shoes instead! It could be used as a pretty bag to carry your books in as well.

1. Following the appliqué steps shown on page 10, create the shoe appliqué design in red floral and silver fabric on the red linen. Add embroidery as described on pages 12–13 and stitch a bow to the shoe front, using the photograph opposite as a guide for position.

2. Apply Bondaweb to the reverse of the pieces of linen, cord, and the two floral fabrics. Cut each piece into a square 2¼ x 2¼in. (5.5 x 5.5cm) and then in half diagonally to create triangles. Use five triangles of each fabric, 20 triangles in total. Arrange the triangles to make a border above and below the shoe appliqué panel. Peel off the Bondaweb backing and iron in place. Zigzag stitch around the edges of the triangles.

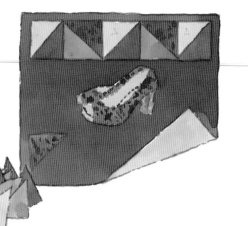

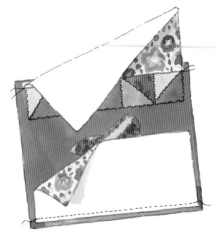

3. From the laminated floral fabric cut two side panels each 2½ x 18in. (6.5 x 45cm), top and bottom panels each 11 x 5in. (27.5 x 12.5cm) and a back piece 14½ x 18in. (36.5 x 45cm). With right sides together, machine stitch the top and bottom panels to the shoe appliqué panel using a ⅝in. (15mm) seam. Open out. Add the two side panels either side in the same way.

Materials

Shoe template on page 123

10 x 12in. (25 x 30cm) piece of red linen fabric

4 x 4in. (10 x 10cm) pieces of red floral fabric

2 x 4in. (5 x 10cm) pieces of silver fabric

12 x 12in. (30 x 30cm) piece of Bondaweb

Coordinating pearl embroidery floss

Embroidery hoop

Ribbon bow

Bugle beads and sequins

2½ x 7in. (6.5 x 17.5cm) each of purple linen, lilac baby cord, and red floral fabrics

5 x 24in. (12.5 x 60cm) piece of orange floral fabric

20 x 32in. (50 x 80cm) piece of laminated floral fabric

4 large pearl buttons

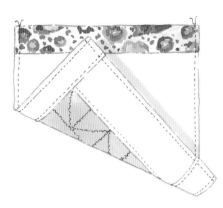

4. Fold the top edge of the bag over to neaten. Place the front of the bag right sides together to the back and turn over the top of the back to match the front. Machine stitch around the sides and bottom of the bag. Turn right side out.

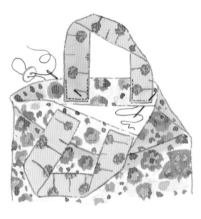

5. Cut two 16 x 5in. (40 x 12.5cm) strips of orange floral fabric. Fold each in half lengthwise, right sides facing, and stitch into a tube. Turn right side out and press. Pin the end of each bag handle to the top edge of the bag and hand sew onto the inner folded hem. Stitch a large button through all layers over where the straps are attached, to reinforce the stitching.

Coin purse

This glitzy, girly purse is made from a silk base and decorated with a beautiful selection of patterned and plain fabrics, plus beads, sequins, and buttons. You could adapt the design to use different shapes and make the embellishment as intricate or simple as you like—just play around with the idea.

Materials

12 x 8in. (30 x 20cm) piece of silver silk fabric

12 x 12in. (30 x 30cm) piece of felt

Scraps of mint green polka, floral, and pink fabrics

4 x 8in. (10 x 20cm) piece of Bondaweb

Flower templates on page 124

Selection of buttons, beads, and sequins

Coordinating pearl embroidery floss

Embroidery hoop

Coordinating 6in. (15cm) zipper

14in. (35cm) narrow pink ribbon

Butterfly template on page 120

1. Cut two pieces of silver silk fabric and two pieces of felt, each measuring 6 x 8in. (15 x 20cm). Following the appliqué steps shown on page 10, create the flower appliqué design in colored scraps on one piece of the silver silk fabric. Add embroidery, beading, and buttons as described on pages 12–13, using the photograph opposite as a guide.

2. Turn over ⅝in. (15mm) along the top edge of each silk piece. Place the folded edges over the zipper with the fold close to the zipper teeth on each side. Tack the zipper in place and then machine stitch.

3. Turn the purse over and position the two pieces of felt lining on the wrong side of the silk pieces, tucking the top edge under the zipper tape. Slip stitch or work running stitch along the zipper tape to hold the felt in place, being careful not to stitch through to the silk layer.

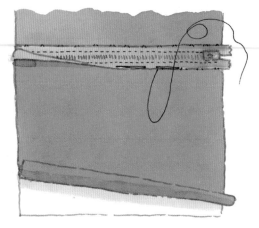

4. Fold the purse right sides together, leaving the zipper slightly open. Pin and machine stitch around the sides and bottom. Trim the seams, open the zipper, and turn the purse right side out. Cut a 6in. (15cm) length of ribbon and tie it to the zipper pull.

5. Back a scrap of pink silk with felt using Bondaweb. Copy the butterfly template onto this and cut out the shape. Hand stitch in place at the top right hand corner of the purse. Embellish with sequins, then make a bow with the remaining ribbon and stitch in place.

Chapter 5

Cute Clothes & Accessories

Baby shoes

Dog coat

Evening bag

Appliqué top

Denim skirt

Make-up bag

Appliqué embellished skirt

Sequined hair band

Yo-yo jewelry

Baby shoes

These baby shoes are seriously cute! They are made using a simple pattern and can be embellished with embroidery, motifs, beads, and sequins. Use the pattern as it is to make a beautiful pair of soft shoes for a new baby or reduce or enlarge for dolly shoes and toddler slippers.

Materials

8 x 8in. (20 x 20cm) piece of small floral print fabric

8 x 14in. (20 x 35cm) piece of Bondaweb

8 x 14in. (20 x 35cm) piece of cotton batting (wadding)

6 x 6in. (15 x 15cm) piece of large floral print fabric

Baby shoe templates on page 124

Coordinating pearl embroidery floss

Coordinating beads and sequins

8in. (20cm) of lace trimming

Eyelet punch

24in. (60cm) of narrow ribbon

1. Cut a piece of Bondaweb 8 x 8in. (20 x 20cm) and iron onto the wrong side of the small floral print fabric. Peel away the paper backing. Cut an 8 x 8in. (20 x 20cm) piece of cotton batting (wadding) and place on top of the Bondaweb layer and then iron until all layers are fixed together. Repeat using the piece of large floral print fabric.

2. Copy the baby shoe templates twice, flipping the sole piece so you have right and left to make one set for each foot. Pin the templates for the top of the shoes to the small floral print fabric, positioning them to use the motifs in the design. Pin the templates for the soles to the large floral print fabric. Cut out all the pieces.

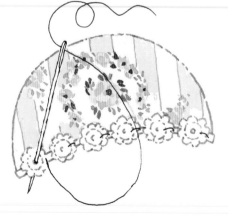

3. Work simple hand embroidery into the floral pattern on the front top piece of the baby shoe and add coordinating beads and sequins, following the instructions on pages 12–13. Hand stitch a length of lace trimming along the top edge of each of the front pieces.

4. Pin the back and then the front of each shoe onto the sole. Work blanket stitch around the edge of each sole to hold all the pieces of the shoe together.

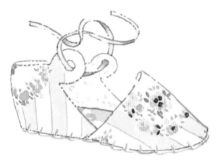

5. Cut the length of ribbon in half. Using the eyelet punch, cut a small hole in the tip on either side of the shoe backs and thread a length of ribbon through the holes. Tie the ribbon in a pretty bow.

Dog coat

Is your dog a trend setter? If so, then have a go at making this patterned patchwork dog coat. Embellished with a decorative floral corsage, it is guaranteed to get your doggy strutting her stuff.

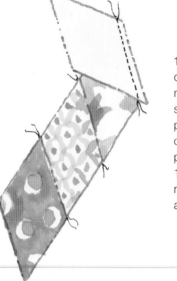

1. Using the diamond template, mark out and cut six diamonds from each of the four coordinating fabrics, making 24 diamonds in total. Using a ¼in. (5mm) seam, stitch the diamonds together in rows, and then press the seams to one side in alternate directions on each row. Stitch the rows together to make a piece of patchwork fabric measuring approx. 16 x 16in. (40 x 40cm). For a larger dog you will need to increase the size by adding more diamonds, and to increase the size of the coat template.

Materials

12 x 12in. (30 x 30cm) each of four coordinating fabrics

Diamond template on page 125

Dog coat template on page 125

17 x 17in. (42.5 x 42.5cm) piece of striped lining fabric

17 x 17in. (42.5 x 42.5cm) piece of batting (wadding)

Assorted buttons

36in. (90cm) of lilac ribbon

6 x 6in. (15 x 15cm) piece of lilac felt

Petal template on page 125

6 x 6in. (15 x 15cm) piece of Bondaweb

5 beads

Large snap fastener (press stud)

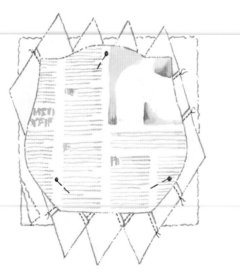

2. Measure the dog and enlarge the coat template on page 125 to fit, making a paper pattern from newspaper. Place the lining fabric wrong side up with the batting (wadding) on top and then add the patchwork panel right side up. Pin on the paper pattern and cut out the shapes through all layers.

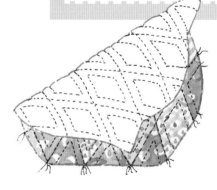

3. Remove the lining fabric and stitch along the seams of the diamonds to quilt the patchwork to the batting (wadding). Add a second line of machine quilt stitching within each diamond, parallel to the seamline. Stitch on the buttons at random intervals to embellish the patchwork piece.

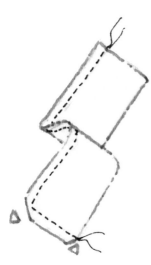

4. For the strap cut a piece of fabric 8 x 5in. (20 x 12.5cm) and fold in half lengthwise with right sides facing. Machine stitch the long edge and across one short edge. Trim seams and across corners, turn right side out, and press.

5. Place the strap on the right side of the coat with the raw edges of coat and strap aligned and the strap lying toward the center. Place the lining on top with right side facing the patchwork panel. Machine stitch around the edge, using a ⅝in. (15mm) seam allowance and leaving the top open for turning. Turn right side out.

6. Cut the ribbon in half and insert the ends into either side at the front of the dog coat. Turn under the front edge by approx. ¼in. (5mm) and slip stitch closed, catching the ribbons in place.

7. Fold back the collar and hand stitch in place. Add a row of buttons for additional decoration.

8. Bond some of the larger leftover pieces of fabric to the piece of felt using Bondaweb and cut out five petal shapes using the petal template. Fold one end over crossways and then fold the petal in half along the length. Stitch the short folded edges together to make a flower using the photograph opposite as a guide. Embellish the flower with beads and a decorative button. Hand stitch it to the coat near the collar. Measure the strap around the dog and stitch the snap fastener (press stud) onto the strap and coat to fit.

Evening bag

I really enjoy making accessories and I always receive lovely compliments about my little bags, so I thought it would be good to include a simple bag for you to try. If you have a small piece of stunning fabric, but can't think of a way to display it, use it as an accent as I've done in this design.

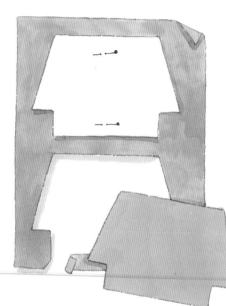

1. Cut a 14 x 18in. (35 x 45cm) piece of lilac cotton fabric. Place this wrong side upward and iron a piece of Bondaweb on top. Peel off the backing and then add a layer of lining fabric and iron in place. Place the bag template onto the layered fabric, draw around it and cut out the front and back bag pieces.

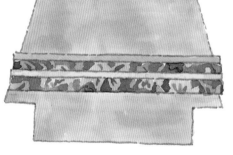

2. Cut one 2 x 12in. (5 x 30cm) strip of floral fabric. Iron Bondaweb to the reverse and to the reverse of the strips of blue and yellow silk. Apply the three strips to the front bag piece, using the photograph opposite as a guide for positioning. Set the machine to an open zigzag stitch and stitch along the edge of each strip to finish.

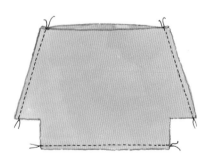

3. Place the front and back of the bag together right sides facing and machine stitch down the sides and along the bottom only, using a ⅝in. (15mm) seam and leaving corner angles unstitched as shown. Press seams flat. To create the base corner gusset, pull the front and back of the bag apart and then flatten the bag the other way so the side seam and bottom seams lie over one another, which pulls the corner angle into a straight line. Stitch across the corner. Repeat on the other side, then turn the bag right side out.

Materials

14 x 22in. (35 x 55cm) piece of lilac cotton fabric

14 x 24in. (35 x 60cm) piece of Bondaweb

14 x 18in. (35 x 45cm) piece of lining fabric

Bag template on page 125

14 x 22in. (35 x 55cm) piece of floral fabric

¾ x 12in. (1.5 x 30cm) piece of blue silk fabric

½ x 12in. (1 x 30cm) piece of yellow silk fabric

8 x 16in. (20 x 40cm) piece of fusible interfacing

Button

Snap fastener (press stud)

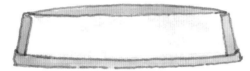

4. Use the facing template to cut two facing pieces from the remaining lilac cotton fabric. Place the facing pieces right sides together and machine down the short sides to join, using a ⅝in. (15mm) seam. Turn over by ¼in. (5mm) along the longer edge and press.

5. Pin the facing around the top of the bag with right sides facing and with the narrower edge toward the top. Machine stitch around the top about ¼in. (5mm) from the edge and then fold the facing over to the inside, leaving a narrow band showing on the front. Work slip stitch around the facing on the inside of the bag to hold it in place, making sure the stitching does not show on the front.

6. For the strap cut a 4 x 12in. (10 x 30cm) length of floral fabric and iron the fusible interfacing onto the wrong side. Fold the strap in half lengthwise with right sides facing and machine stitch along the length. Turn the tube right side out. Press the strap so the seam runs down the center of the width.

7. Pin the bag strap in place on each side of the top, folding each end under by ¼in. (5mm) to neaten raw edges. Back stitch by hand to the inside of the bag to hold the strap in place, making sure the stitches do not show on the front.

8. Using the remaining floral fabric, make a large yo-yo (Suffolk puff) as described on page 11. Stitch onto the front of the bag at the top corner. Add the button in the center. Stitch a snap fastener (press stud) inside the bag to close it.

Appliqué top

Embellishing and customizing clothing is one of my favorite techniques. Plain tops can easily be turned into unique statement pieces with some clever appliqué and embroidery. You could also use the templates provided to add detail to skirts and jeans—the possibilities are endless!

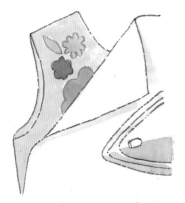

1. Following the appliqué steps shown on page 10, create the floral appliqué design in green and lilac fabrics on the sleeveless top, using the photograph opposite as a guide for positioning.

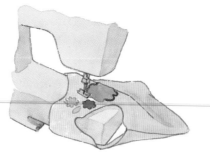

2. Set the sewing machine to a close zigzag and machine stitch all around the edge of some of the flower shapes, using a coordinating color sewing thread. Add hand embroidery to the flower shapes and add beads, sequins, and buttons to the design, following the instructions on pages 12–13 and using the photograph opposite as a guide.

3. To make the contrast border, measure the width across the hem of the sleeveless top and cut two lengths of dotted fabric, each the same measurement plus 1¼in. (3cm) for seam allowances and 3in (7.5cm) wide. Place the two pieces with right sides facing, and machine stitch across the short ends on either side. Press the seams open.

4. Turn over along one long edge of the border by ¼in. (5cm) twice, press the folds in place, and slip stitch the hem. With right sides facing slide the border onto the sleeveless top, aligning the unhemmed edge with the top's hem. Pin and machine stitch in place. Fold the edging down and press seams.

Materials

Plain sleeveless top

Appliqué template on page 126

Small pieces of green and lilac fabrics

6 x 6in. (15 x 15cm) piece of Bondaweb

Coordinating machine thread

Coordinating embroidery floss

Embroidery hoop

Selection of buttons, beads, and sequins

Approx. 3 x 30in. (7.5 x 75cm) piece of lilac dotted fabric

Denim skirt

Recycle, recycle, recycle! There is no need to throw away old jeans anymore—with a couple of strips of fabric and some decorative buttons you can transform them into a sweet little ra-ra skirt.

1. Cut the legs off the denim jeans just under the back pockets and open up the inner leg seam around the crotch area. Cut away any excess fabric around the crotch so the skirt lies flat. Measure the gaps left at the base of the skirt at front and back and cut two triangles to match from the trouser legs, allowing ¼in. (5mm) extra along both sides for seams.

2. Place one of the triangles under the gap at the front to fill it, turning under the raw edges of the upper layer and pinning in place. Machine stitch around the sides of the triangle and press flat. Repeat with the other triangle to fill the gap at the back.

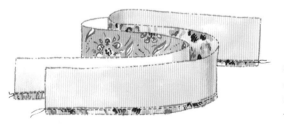

3. The two lengths of floral fabric will form the ruffles (frills). Hem along one long edge of each by turning under by ¼in. (5mm) and then by ½in. (12mm) and topstitching in place on the machine.

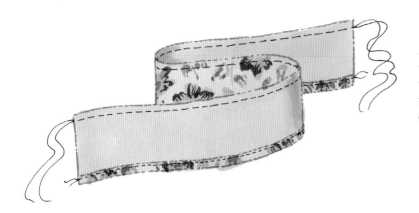

4. To gather the ruffles (frills) set the sewing machine to the longest stitch length and machine stitch along the unhemmed long edge of each of the lengths of fabric. Do not back stitch at the seam ends and leave excess thread at each end for gathering.

5. Knot the two threads at one end together. Hold one of the threads at the other end and ease the fabric along its entire length to gather until it will fit around the base of the denim skirt. Knot the threads at the other end to keep the gathers in place and then even them out along the ruffle (frill). Repeat for the other floral ruffle (frill).

6. Fold each ruffle (frill) in half with wrong sides together and stitch across the short ends with a ¼in. (5mm) seam to make each into a circle. Press the seam open, turn right side out. Pin the wider ruffle (frill) onto the bottom of the skirt and machine stitch in place. Pin on the narrower ruffle (frill) so it overlaps the top of the lower frill. Machine stitch, and then trim any excess fabric away above the stitching line.

Tip

The depth of the lower frill sets the final length of the skirt, so if you want the skirt longer make this frill a little deeper.

7. For the gingham ribbon ruffle (frill), cut a 36in. (90cm) length of ribbon. Set the machine to its longest stitch again and machine stitch along the center of the ribbon. Gather as explained in step 5. Pin the gathered gingham ribbon onto the skirt to cover the raw edge at the top of the upper frill, turning the ends of the ribbon under to neaten them, and then hand stitch in place.

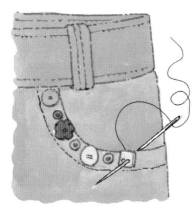

8. For the final decoration make a bow with the remaining gingham ribbon and stitch in place. Sew on a selection of buttons and sequins around the pocket area and onto the ribbon ruffle (frill) with a length of embroidery floss, using the photograph (right) as a guide.

Make-up bag

This project takes inspiration from the Union Jack flag. The use of pretty and delicate floral fabrics and coordinating silks give it a shabby chic feel. Make it for yourself or to give as a gorgeous gift.

1. Cut two 10 x 12½in. (25 x 32cm) pieces of floral fabric and two of lining fabric for the base of the bag. For the Union Jack design cut two 1¼ x 16in. (3 x 40cm) strips of floral fabric, one 2 x 16in. (5 x 40cm) strip of floral fabric, one 2 x 14in. (5 x 35cm) strip of floral fabric, two 1¼ x 16in. (3 x 40cm) strips of turquoise dotted fabric, one 1¼ x 10in. (3 x 25cm) strip of blue silk fabric and one 1¼ x 14in. (3 x 35cm) strip of blue silk fabric.

2. Apply Bondaweb to the back of all the strips. Peel off the backing. Arrange the strips into the Union Jack design on one of the pieces of floral fabric, using the photograph opposite as a guide, and iron in place. Set the machine to an open zigzag stitch and machine stitch around the lines of the design. Trim off pieces that extend over the edges of the base fabric.

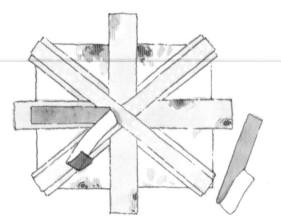

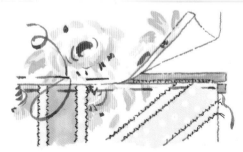

3. On both pieces of floral fabric and the lining pieces turn under ⅝in. (1.5cm) along the shorter top edge and press. Place the zipper right side up and place the floral fabric pieces on either side, right side up, with the folded edge close to the zipper teeth. Baste (tack) the zipper in place and then machine stitch.

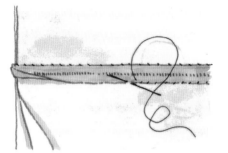

4. Turn the floral section over. Position the two pieces of lining on top of the floral pieces, right side up, with the folded edge close to the zipper teeth. Slip stitch along the zipper tape to hold the lining in place.

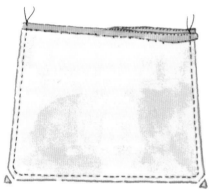

5. Fold the make-up bag right sides together leaving the zip slightly open. Pin and machine stitch around the bag. Clip off corners and trim seams, being careful not to cut through the stitching.

6. Open the zipper and turn the bag right side out. Stitch one of the tiny buttons to the center of the front.

7. Use a piece of Bondaweb to bond a scrap of blue silk to a piece of pink felt. Cut a small heart shape from the silk/felt and another from plain felt. Stitch the remaining two buttons to the plain felt heart. Place the heart pieces together, right side outward, and work blanket stitch around the edges leaving a gap for the filling. Make a bow in blue ribbon and stitch to the front of the heart.

8. Stuff the heart. Thread the length of pink ribbon through the zipper pull and push the raw ends into the stuffed heart. Close the gap with running stitch.

Appliqué embellished skirt

If you have an old skirt that has started to look tired, this project shows you how to update it with simple appliqué and ribbon trim for a gorgeous new look.

Materials

Flower spray template on page 126

Scraps of coordinating fabrics

12 x 12in. (30 x 30cm) piece of Bondaweb

Plain skirt to customize

Coordinating pearl embroidery floss

Embroidery hoop

Coordinating beads and sequins

Approx. 90in. (225cm) matching ribbon

1. Lay out the selection of fabrics and decide which ones go well together. Following the appliqué steps as shown on page 10, create the flower appliqué design near the hem of the skirt.

2. Add hand embroidery to the flowers, using chain stitch, back stitch, running stitch, and French knots as described on page 12 and following the photograph opposite as a guide.

3. Add a selection of beads, sequins, and buttons as described on page 13.

4. Pin a length of ribbon around just above the hem of the skirt and stitch in place with an open zigzag stitch.

Sequined hair band

If you are new to sewing and are just beginning to use a sewing machine, I would recommend this project as a good place to start. It is a quick, simple to stitch, and uses a minimal amount of materials.

Materials

2½ x 12in. (6.5 x 30cm) each of pink dotted and floral fabrics

3 x 2in. (7.5 x 5cm) piece of coral pink cotton

Pink sequins and beads

36in. (90cm) of pink ribbon

Hair band

Hot glue gun

1. Place the dotted and floral fabrics with right sides facing and machine stitch along the top and bottom edges. Turn right side out and press so that the seams run down the middle on each side.

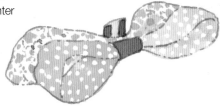

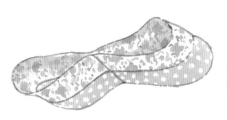

2. Fold each end underneath to the center, gather together and stitch in place by hand.

3. Take the piece of coral fabric and press each side under to hide the raw edges. Wrap it around the center of the bow and hand stitch in place at the back.

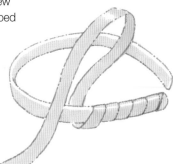

4. Decorate the bow with a few sequins and beads, as described on page 13.

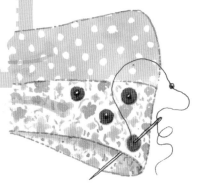

5. Wind the pink ribbon around the hair band to cover it, using the hot glue gun to secure the ends in place. Use the hot glue gun to attach the bow onto the hair band.

Yo-yo jewelry

Yo-yos (or Suffolk puffs) are extremely versatile and can be used in many different ways. To create this elegant necklace design, I made a selection of yo-yos in different sizes using various silks. When beaded and strung together, they make a unique statement necklace—perfect for any occasion.

1. Iron a piece of Bondaweb on the wrong side of the green silk fabric and then remove the paper backing and lay the green spotty fabric wrong side down on top. Iron to bond the layers. Repeat with the yellow silk and yellow floral fabrics.

2. On the layered green silk, draw and cut one circle 4in. (10cm) in diameter and two circles 2in. (5cm) in diameter. On the layered yellow silk draw and cut two circles 3in. (7.5cm) in diameter.

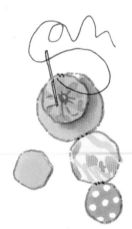

3. Following the instructions on page 11, make each of the circles into a yo-yo (Suffolk puff). Stitch the yo-yos together at the edges as shown in the photograph.

4. Stitch a heart-shape button in between each yo-yo and apply beads to the center of each. Attach the beading thread to one end, and thread beads to the desired length. Add one half of the necklace fastening. Repeat on the other side.

Materials

5 x 9in. (12.5 x 22.5cm) piece of green silk fabric

9 x 9in. (22.5 x 22.5cm) piece of green dotted silk fabric

4 x 7in. (10 x 17.5cm) piece of yellow silk fabric

7 x 7in. (17.5 x 17.5cm) piece of yellow floral fabric

16 x 16in. (40 x 40cm) piece of Bondaweb

4 heart shaped buttons

Assorted small beads

15in. (37.5cm) of bead thread

1 set of necklace fastenings

Templates

Crib quilt (page 16)

Stuffed dolly (page 24)

Heart:
ACTUAL SIZE

Butterfly:
ACTUAL SIZE

Flower:
ACTUAL SIZE

Arm:
ACTUAL SIZE

Leg:
ACTUAL SIZE

Star:
ACTUAL SIZE

Skirt:
ENLARGE 200%

Flower:
ACTUAL SIZE

Stuffed dolly (page 24)

Unicorn pillow (page 30)

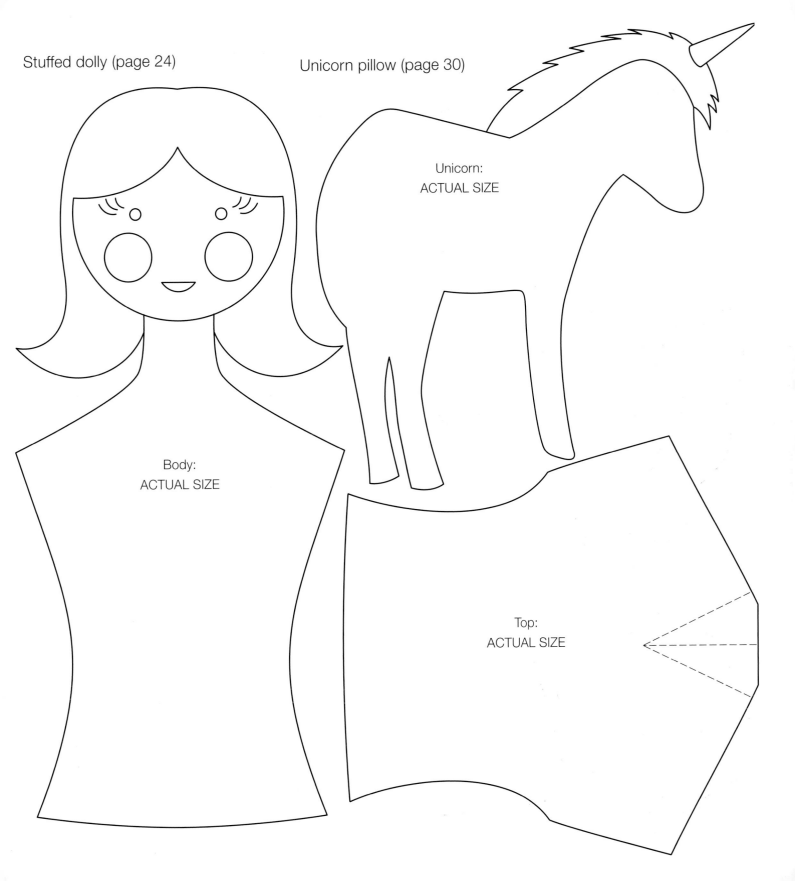

Unicorn:
ACTUAL SIZE

Body:
ACTUAL SIZE

Top:
ACTUAL SIZE

Pajama bag (page 34)

Small butterfly:
ACTUAL SIZE

Medium butterfly:
ACTUAL SIZE

Large butterfly:
ACTUAL SIZE

Egg cozy (page 40)

Egg cozy:
ACTUAL SIZE

Octagon:
ACTUAL SIZE

Jam pot covers (page 42)

Strawberry:
ACTUAL SIZE

Coffee pot cozy (page 44)

Coffee pot patchwork:
ACTUAL SIZE

Coffee pot cupcake:
ACTUAL SIZE

Teapot cozy tea cup:
ACTUAL SIZE

Teapot picture
(page 50)

Teapot:
ENLARGE 200%

Teapot cozy (page 60)

Teapot cozy:
ENLARGE 200%

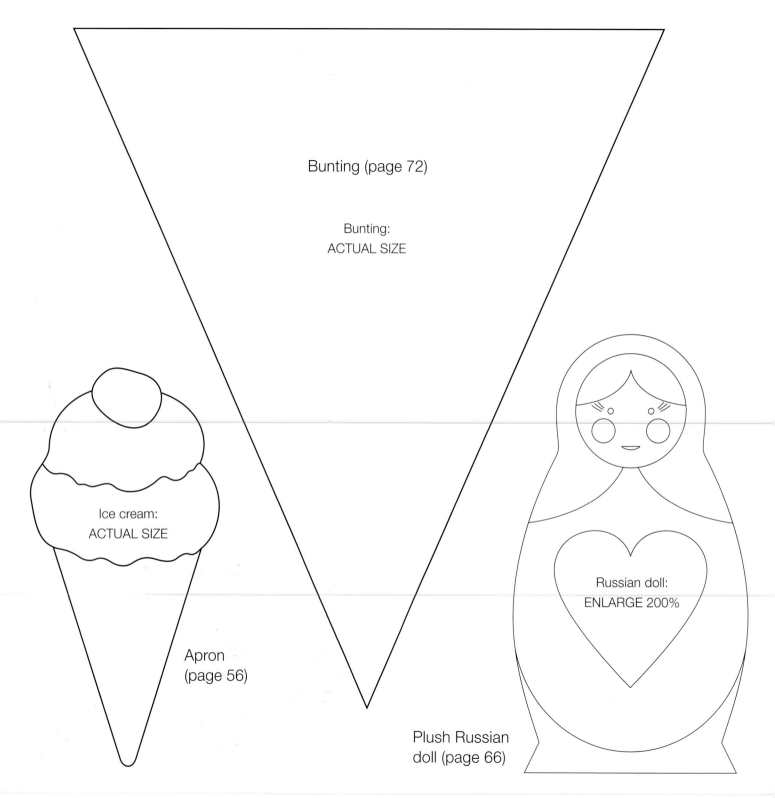

Bunting (page 72)

Bunting:
ACTUAL SIZE

Ice cream:
ACTUAL SIZE

Apron
(page 56)

Russian doll:
ENLARGE 200%

Plush Russian
doll (page 66)

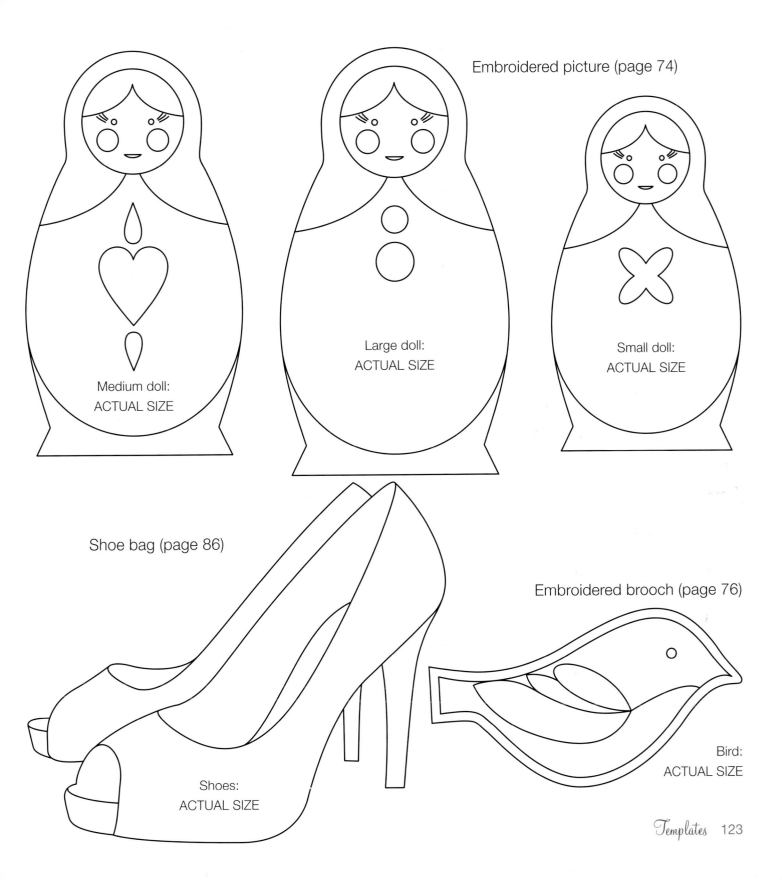

Embroidered picture (page 74)

Medium doll:
ACTUAL SIZE

Large doll:
ACTUAL SIZE

Small doll:
ACTUAL SIZE

Shoe bag (page 86)

Embroidered brooch (page 76)

Shoes:
ACTUAL SIZE

Bird:
ACTUAL SIZE

Flower 1:
ACTUAL SIZE

Coin purse (page 88)

Flower 2:
ACTUAL SIZE

Flower group:
ACTUAL SIZE

Baby shoes (page 92)

Shoe back:
ACTUAL SIZE

Shoe sole:
ACTUAL SIZE

Shoe front:
ACTUAL SIZE

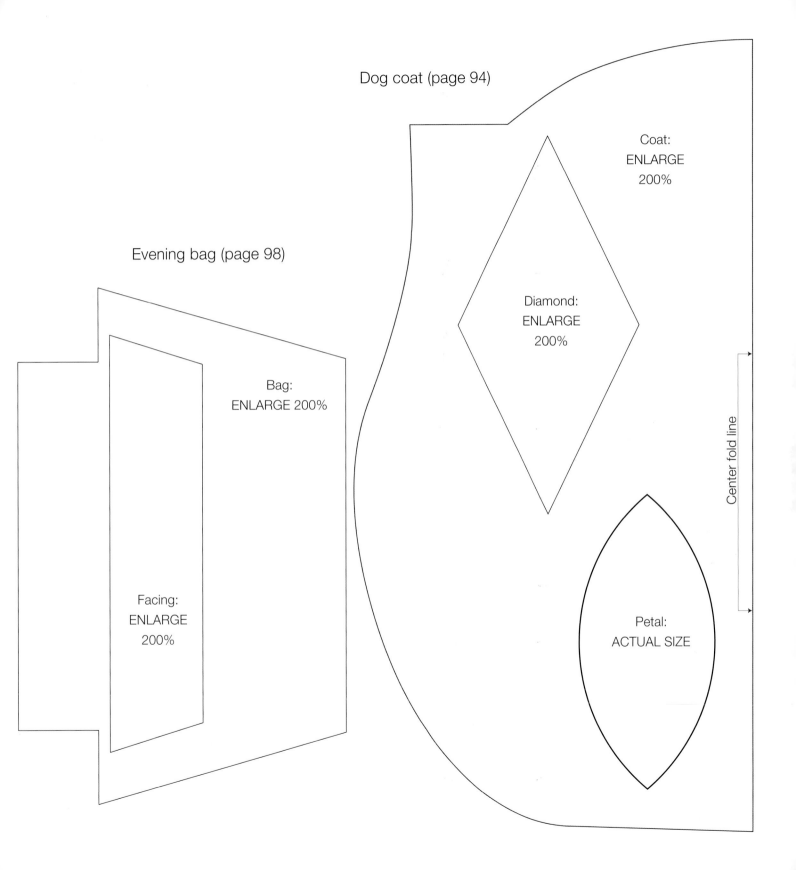

Dog coat (page 94)

Evening bag (page 98)

Coat:
ENLARGE
200%

Diamond:
ENLARGE
200%

Bag:
ENLARGE 200%

Facing:
ENLARGE
200%

Petal:
ACTUAL SIZE

Center fold line

Appliqué top (page 102)

Pattern:
ENLARGE 200%

Flower Spray:
ACTUAL SIZE

Appliqué embellished
skirt (page 112)

Make-up bag
(page 108)

Heart:
ACTUAL SIZE

Suppliers

North America

A.C. Moore
Stores nationwide
1-888-226-6673
www.acmoore.com

Amy Butler
www.amybutler.com

B.B. Bargoons
8201 Keele Street
Concord, ON L4K 1Z4
1-800-665-9227
www.bbbargoons.com

Britex Fabrics
146 Geary Street
San Francisco, CA 94108
415-392-2910
www.britexfabrics.com

Buy Fabrics
8967 Rand Ave
Daphne, Al 36526
877-625-2889
www.buyfabrics.com

Cia's Palette
4155 Grand Ave S
Minneapolis, MN 55409
612-229-5227
www.ciaspalette.com

Crafts, etc.
1-800-888-0321
www.craftsetc.com
Online store.

Denver Fabrics
10490 Baur Blvd. St.
St. Louis, MO 63132
1-800-468-0602
www.denverfabrics.com

Discount Fabrics USA
108 N. Carroll St.
Thurmont, MD 21788
301-271-2266
www.discountfabricsusa
corp.com

FabDir.com
www.fabdir.com
The Internet's largest
fabric store directory.

Fabricland/Fabricville
www.fabricland.com
www.fabricville.com
Over 170 stores in
Canada.

J & O Fabrics
9401 Rt. 130
Pennsauken, NJ 08110
856-663-2121
www.jandofabrics.com

Hobby Lobby
Stores nationwide
www.hobbylobby.com

**Jo-Ann Fabric and
Craft Store**
1-888-739-4120
www.joann.com
Stores nationwide.

Lucy's Fabrics
103 S. College Street
Anna, TX 75409
866-544-5829
www.lucysfabrics.com

Michaels
1-800-642-4235
www.michaels.com
Stores nationwide.

Purl Patchwork
147 Sullivan Street
New York, NY 10012
00 1 212 420 8798
www.purlsoho.com

Reprodepot Fabrics
413-527-4047
www.reprodepotfabrics.
com

**Tinsel Trading
Company**
47 West 38th Street
New York, NY 10018
212-730-1030
www.tinseltrading.com

Vogue Fabrics
718-732 Main Street
Evanston, IL 60202
847-864-9600
www.voguefabricstore.com

Wazoodle
2–9 Heritage Road
Markham, ON L3P 1M3
1-866-473-4628
www.wazoodle.com

Z and S Fabrics
681 S. Muddy Creek
Road
Denver, PA 17157
717-336-4026
www.zandsfabrics.com

UK

**Abakhan Fabrics,
Hobby, and Home**
Stores across north-west
England and Wales
www.abakhan.co.uk

Borovick's
16 Berwick Street
London W1F 0HP
020 7437 2180
www.borovickfabrics
ltd.co.uk

The Cloth House
47 Berwick Street
London W1F 8SJ
020 7437 5155
www.clothhouse.com

Coats Crafts
Green Lane Mill
Holmfirth
West Yorkshire
HD9 2DX
01484 681881
www.coatscrafts.co.uk

The Cotton Patch
1283-1285 Stratford Rd
Hall Green, Birmingham
B28 9AJ
0121 702 2840
www.cottonpatch.co.uk

Fabric Galore
52–54 Lavender Hill
Battersea
London
SW115RH

Fabric Land
52-56 Bond Street
Bristol
BS1 3L2
0117 922 0500
www.fabricland.co.uk

Hobby Craft
Stores nationwide
01202 596100
www.hobbycraft.co.uk

John Lewis
Stores nationwide
www.johnlewis.com

Liberty
Regent Street
London W1
020 7734 1234
www.liberty.co.uk

The Make Lounge
49–51 Barnsbury Street
London N1 1PT
020 7609 0275
www.themakelounge.com

Mandors
Stores in Glasgow and
Edinburgh
0141 332 7716
www.mandors.co.uk

The Sewing Box
50 Newgate Street
Morpeth, Northumberland
NE61 1BE
01670 511171
www.sewing-box.co.uk

VV Rouleaux
102 Marylebone Lane
London W1U 2QD
020 7224 5179
www.vvrouleaux.com

Index